**MagicImage Filmbooks
Presents**

FRANKENSTEIN MEETS THE WOLF MAN

(The Original Shooting Script)

Edited by Philip J. Riley

Foreword by Curt Siodmak

Production Background by Gregory Wm. Mank

Atlantic City · Hollywood

**UNIVERSAL FILMSCRIPTS SERIES
CLASSIC HORROR FILMS - VOLUME 5**

1279-4690

Frankenstein Meets the Wolf Man
(The Original Shooting Script)

FIRST EDITION

Published by MagicImage Filmbooks, 740 S. 6th Avenue, Absecon, NJ 08201

The Library of Congress Cataloging in Publication Data:

Siodmak, Curt, 1902-
    [Frankenstein Meets the Wolf Man]
    MagicImage Filmbooks presents Frankenstein Meets the Wolf Man :
the original 1942 shooting script / edited by Philip J. Riley ;
foreword by Curt Siodmak ; production background by Gregory Wm.
Mank. -- 1st ed.
    p. cm. -- (Universal filmscripts series. Classic horror
films ; v. 5)
    1. Frankenstein (Fictitious character)--Drama. 2. Frankenstein
Meets the Wolf Man (Motion picture) 3. Frankenstein films.
I. Riley, Philip J., 1948- . II. Mank, Gregory W.
III. MagicImage Filmbooks (Firm) IV. Frankenstein Meets the Wolf
Man. V. Series.
PN1997.F685 1990
791.43'72--dc20   90-61037
                                        CIP

ISBN: 1-882127-13-7

10 9 8 7 6 5 4 3 2 1

The purpose of this series is the preservation of the art of writing for the screen. Rare books have long been a source of enjoyment and an investment for the serious collector, and even in limited printings there usually were a few thousand produced. Scripts, however, numbered only 50 at the most, and we are proud to present them in their original form. Some will be final shooting scripts and some earlier drafts, so that students, libraries, archives and film-lovers might, for the first time, study them in their original form. In producing these volumes, we hope that the unique art of screenplay writing will be preserved for future generations.

1279-25AA.

CREDITS AND ACKNOWLEDGMENTS

A Michael D. Stein Production

Editor, Philip J. Riley

Art Director, Marisa Donato-Riley

Artists, Robert Semler, A.S.I.
           Marisa Donato-Riley

Creative Consultant, Andrew Lee, Head of Research,
Universal Studios (retired)

Editorial Assistant, Janet Stein

Cover - Courtesy Cinema Collectors, Hollywood, CA
Pressbook - Courtesy Richard Bojarski Collection

The author wishes to thank the following individuals
and institutions for their generous assistance:

Ronald V. Borst   Urbano Lemus
James Cerone   Linda Mehr
Ned Comstock   John Poorman
Nancy Cushing-Jones   Anne Schlosser
Sue Dwiggins   Michael Sington
Rita Duenas   David Skal
Donald Fowle   Viviana Strahl
Robert Furmanek   Ron Stransky
Eric Hoffman   Dorothy Swerdlove
Maria Jochsberger   Wallace Worsley
Yvon Kartak

THE BILLY ROSE THEATER COLLECTION,
New York Public Library, Lincoln Ctr., New York City

THE MARGARET HERRICK LIBRARY,
Academy of Motion Picture Arts and Sciences

USC ARCHIVES OF PERFORMING ARTS
SPECIAL COLLECTIONS

Manufactured in the United States of America

Typesetting by Computer House, Absecon, New Jersey

Printed and bound by
McNaughton & Gunn Lithographers

Dedicated to:

Curt Siodmak, a man who is pure at heart
and says his prayers at night

and to:

his beautiful wife (and great cook) Henrietta
&
their Christmas tree

Curt Siodmak and Philip J. Riley with Henrietta's invisible
Christmas tree in the background, 1989.

Foreword
By
Curt Siodmak

*A small selection of books and scenes from the works of Curt Siodmak: Robert Florey and
Peter Lorre on the set of THE BEAST WITH FIVE FINGERS, and Lon Chaney Jr. in SON OF DRACULA.*

The film's title is a misnomer. Logically, it should have been *The Frankenstein Monster Meets the Wolf Man*. But that was too long a title for the publicity department, nor did it have the pizazz a title needs to lure people into the cinema. That was the belief of the publicity department, which is paid to feel the pulse of the public, though titles rarely sell tickets.

But in the case of *Frankenstein Meets the Wolf Man*, I have to take the blame, since the title is based on a joke I made (which taught me never to crack a bad joke in a film studio - the producers might see a picture in it, and the writer will be faced with the choice of writing a story around it or not collecting a weekly salary). Since we writers lived from one weekly check to the next, an assignment was the time between two lay-offs. In the forties, at the crest of the horror picture productions, we poets got paid for our working at the studios, like bricklayers or carpenters.

One night, when I was working late at the studio, since the heat in the valley in daytime numbed my brain, a new sound stage was erected opposite my bungalow. In daytime, I used to sit clad only in my jockey shorts at the typewriter, a block of ice and a fan behind it, my secretary stripped to her bra. That was the working arrangement before they invented air conditioning for battleships. Now the public has the advantage of that invention. A hardhat watched me leaving the night-cool bunglow and asked my profession. "A writer?" he said, "working at night? Do you get time and a half overtime?"

Since writers were paid like laborers, the copyright of their output belongs to the studios for eternity. Those pictures made immense profits. Should any of those films become a 'cult picture,' its lifespan outlived that of the producers, directors and writers. Sometimes even the studio. But we writers didn't fight that monopoly, and should we have, there was no chance ever of getting a percentage of the earnings from the studio. That's why no screen writer of the forties ever got wealthy and financially secure, if he didn't also write novels or had success with a stage play. I don't know of any millionaire screenplay authors, though I know millionaire actors, and producers with yachts in the Mediterranean. I believe that since Homer's times, writers are cursed to be underpaid.

I was sitting at the commissary of Universal Studios - a film company for which I wrote two scores of pictures - when my producer George Waggner passed by on his way to the producer's table.

There was a pecking order in the studios, worse than in a chicken den. If one sat at the counter with the grips and electricians, a sandwich was priced at 40 cents. The same sandwich was 45 cents at the table where the secretaries and extras had their luncheon, sixty cents in the Greenroom where the writers ate, and one dollar in the executive room, reserved for directors and producers. But should one be invited to the head of the studio's private dining room, one didn't have to pay at all. Which is a good symbol of the capitalistic system. I never was invited to that room, and sat at the 45 cents hamburger table, since one could invite pretty starlets, who flirted with writers, trying to persuade them to put a juicy, sexy scene for them in the screenplay, which might make them stars, and get them invited to the executive dining room.

Producer George Waggner with Boris Karloff (THE CLIMAX).

When George (for whom I was writing a screenplay, *The Climax,* at that time) walked by my table where I was sitting with Yvonne de Carlo, the most beautiful woman I have ever met, and Mary MacDonald, the most beautiful young woman in the world, I wanted to show off my wit and said:

"George, why don't we make a picture *Frankenstein Wolfs the Meat Man* - I mean, *Frankenstein Meets the Wolf Man.*"

George stopped for a moment, didn't even look at the two enchanting beauties, and didn't smile. I discovered a gleam in his eyes, which I didn't like, because it was not created by the presence of the stunning young women. I laughed, Yvonne laughed, Mary laughed, but not George, who said:

"Is that supposed to be a joke? Then don't put that in my picture."

That was at the time of the Second World War, when America did produce tanks, airplanes and guns, but no automobiles. I needed a car badly, since mine had reached a senile age. A writer friend of mine had a car for sale, a convertible,

handsome Buick. He wanted to get rid of it since he had been drafted. I wanted to buy that car, and confided in George, asking him if I'd get another job when I was through with *The Climax.*

"Buy the car," George said noncommitally. "What's the assignment?" I asked him. "Just buy it, don't worry," George said. That conversation, formulated differently but with the same content, continued for a few days. I couldn't get the answer from him I wanted. He appeared every day in my office asking me if I had bought the Buick. My friend left for the army, and I drained my bank account and bought the car. My conservative wife Henrietta, born and raised in conservative Switzerland, was horrified by the idea of borrowing money from a bank, paying non-productive interest to vile bankers.

"Did you buy the car?" George asked, as every day.

"I did."

"Here's your assignment," George said. *"Frankenstein Meets the Wolf Man."*

"But that was a joke," I answered, startled.

"Not any more," George said," and I give you two hours to come up with a brilliant idea." He didn't say: 'to accept it,' or, 'make up your mind.' He knew he had me over the barrel.

Now I had a Buick convertible, a job to pay for it, and no idea how to write a film with the title *Frankenstein Meets the Wolf Man*. Fortunately, the characters of the two freaks were established. They might contain the 'weenie.' The 'weenie' is the central idea around which the screenplay is written. Larry Talbot (that name which I had given the Wolf Man stuck to him) is aware that at a certain moon phase he was destined to become a murderer. He also had found out that there was no way for him to escape his fate, even if he died, since some mysterious (studio) powers would bring him back to life. But if he could find Baron Victor Frankenstein, who knew the secret of life and death - didn't he construct a body of human parts? - he might learn the answer of how he could escape his horrible fate. On his search for the Baron, he ran into the Frankenstein Monster.

Now, it was the mischievous intention of the screen writer to invent a death for monsters, which makes it very tough for the next writer to find an idea how to bring the monster back to life. The MONSTER had been eradicated in the original Frankenstein picture, burned to ashes. But as was seen in *Frankenstein Meets the Wolf Man*, he still existed, though frozen in perma-ice. He had to be freed from that cold grave, to play his part in the picture. In *Frankenstein Meets the Wolf Man,* he wanted to live, as badly as the Wolf Man wanted to die. The Monster had to find Baron Frankenstein, to keep him alive forever.

One monster wants to die - another one to live forever; that was the 'weenie' which was the pivot of the picture. George bought that idea. Now the rest was the job of constructing situations, scenes, and the continuity to make the story 'believable.'

To find out if my screenplay was carefully scrutinized by the producer, or just after a short perusal turned over to the budget department for the technical and financial breakdown, I usually wrote a scene in it which could easily be deleted. In the screenplay, Larry Talbot, before he again was

8

Universal Studios in 1943 when Curt Siodmak was named "King of the 'B's" by his fellow writers. Today the films are classics, and his name is remembered by thousands of fans while those others writers have, for the most part, disappeared in time.

transfigured into the hairy, terrifying Wolf Man, was dressed in a three piece suit and tie. On his way with the Monster to the Frankenstein Village he turns to the Wolf Man and says:

"You know, I turn into a wolf by night." The Monster's answer is: "Are you kiddin'?" That scene sailed through the front office, but was discovered by my friend Lon Chaney. He thought it wouldn't fit and it was eliminated.

During the shooting I tried to avoid seeing Lon. He went through tortures being physically changed into the Wolf Man. I heard that they nailed him with thin nails to a board, to prevent him from moving even a millimeter out of camera focus during the tedious trick shots. It took almost six hours to make him up and three to take off his gruesome mask. When he caught me in the commissary, where he sat alone due to his horrifying appearance, and where he could only take liquid food through a straw, he glowered at me, mumbling that he would kill me. But I convinced him that he should direct his wrath against Jack Pierce, the genius makeup man and originator of the Frankenstein Monster and the Wolf Man, and not against an innocent writer who had to make a precarious living.

Forty years after the production, I saw the motion picture for the first time. All my life I made it the rule not to see the pictures I had written, since after they had reached the screen, I would think of ideas how to write them better, which is devastatingly depressing.

But the energy and conviction with which Lon played the Monster's part in *Frankenstein Meets the Wolf Man* still exudes from that motion picture. He might have seen in it his own fate: a man driven, searching for a way out of his own despair, remnants of an unhappy childhood which had been deformed by his cruel father, Lon Chaney Sr. But that is a tale I will leave for Phil Riley to write in one of his Lon Chaney Sr.

books. Despite all, Lon Jr. was a wonderful man and a good friend. So - let's all look back to 1942 to see behind the scenes at Universal, during the making of *Frankenstein Meets the Wolf Man* - and then you get to read my script and learn how movies were made, from the written word to the screen.

Curt Siodmak
Three Rivers, California
1989

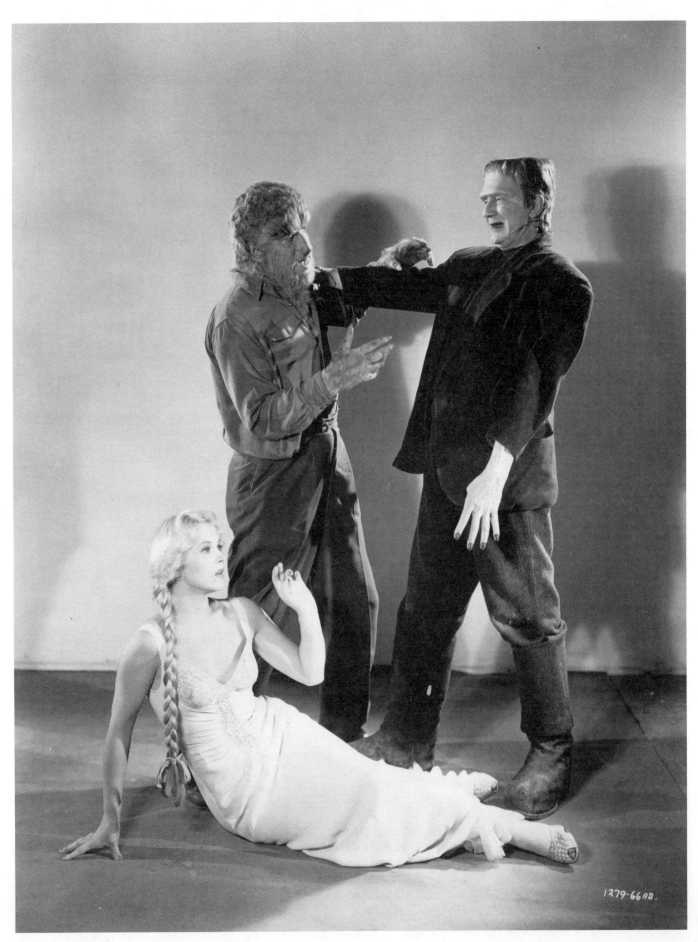

Production Background
By
Gregory Wm. Mank

In 1942, life was full, rich and rewarding for Bela Lugosi.

§

However, during the World War II years, Bela Lugosi was (in the words of his fourth wife, Lillian) "Lord and Master" of his domain - reading his Sociology books, perusing his giant stamp collection, and playing with four year old Bela Jr. And, of course, there were the famous all-night Hungarian parties, where Bela, smoking his ever-present cigar, played the great host as the Bavarian beer and rich wine flowed, and the gypsy musicians played until dawn - at which time Lillian closed the curtains, and the music and festivities went on and on....

Relishing contracts with Universal and Monogram, the immortal star of *Dracula* (1931) was living in his favorite of all his Hollywood homes - 10841 Whipple Street in North Hollywood, neighboring Universal City. It was a Gothic house, complete with a steeple, a giant latticed window, and black ornamental storks atop the roof. Outside, banana trees loomed over the property, and there was a pond; inside, there were a grand piano, a stone Black Forest fireplace, and a great, winding stairway.

"Hollywood" magazine called it "The House That Horror Built. Today, the house is long gone - and apartments stand on the site of what Bela affectionately called his "Dracula House."

The House That Horror Built

Bela Lugosi has been portraying sinister gentle-men on the screen for so long that even his house has absorbed his film personality. Notice the gloomy shadows over the doorway, the leaded windows, the black stork on the housetop. Bela is currently appearing in Monogram's *The Corpse Vanishes*

By HOYT BARNETT

■ *Dracula!* That harbinger of horror, that salacious, sadistic high seer of low slaughter . . .

Who is this sleek, slithering merchant of madness in white tie and tails who kills with a kiss?

Bela Lugosi.

And where does he live?

The North Hollywood real estate board gives the same publicity to his address as it does to earthquakes, for if it were generally known where *Dracula* lives the board fears nearby house-holders might flee the neighborhood and a panic ensue.

But even *Dracula* must live somewhere, and the house in which Lugosi lives fits the character he has made famous on stage and screen as a musty attic fits a spook.

A high brick wall runs around the house, and on top of this wall, embedded in cement, is enough broken glass to cut the pants off a veteran cavalryman. A huge car gate in the wall is studded with heavy bolts, and beside the gate is a dark-stained booth so dim inside that even in broad daylight the single filament bulb casts a glow so low that it but dimly outlines the telephone by which visitors make their presence known.

If you are expected, the suave yet icy voice of Lugosi greets you. A buzz only a little less deadly than the whirr of a rattle snake sounds in the region of your kidneys. Your head pivots toward the sound as a spotlight illuminates a doorknob you have not seen before.

Thrusting this small door open cautiously, you stick your head beyond—for it is better to lose a head than an entire body—and peer into a jungle of banana trees. The cement driveway splits inside the car gate to the left. The little door closes behind you with a click as final as the plop of a guillotine.

You step a few paces to the left and peer along this fork of the concrete drive. A building in the distance, a square jail-like thing, is just right for holding prisoners. So you turn to the right and in the distance is a roof-top sticking above the trees.

Another stride or two and you make out the figures of storks upon the roof, huge, spindly-legged creatures, one poised to fly, another near a nest. To the right is a turret. As you walk toward the house it takes on firmer outlines through the trees.

Huge leaded windows, some of the panes of varied color, give the house an ancient air which is made more ancient still by the low-key of the exterior.

Stepping through the heavy doorway to greet you is a man in shirt sleeves, smoking a heavy pipe. He is taller than six feet and retains the grace of movement coming from well-developed muscles. He smiles slowly, and slowly waves a greeting. He is *Dracula*—no, I mean Lugosi. There is none other with such expressive hands, such mobile features.

"You want to see my house?"

"My summer kitchen." Lugosi points with a householder's pride to a barbecue pit beside a low, square building, one side of which is entirely open. "I like it particularly in the Spring."

We step closer to the main entrance of the house. Now we are beyond the jungle rim. The concrete drives come together here and you see that the building which resembles a jail is in reality a garage.

The house is tall, yet seems to twist and turn as you walk along its front. This effect is due to the design of the entrances, the large central window and the numerous smaller ones made of colored bottle bottoms.

At the left is the secondary entrance, but instead of being a normal doorway it is covered by a roof sloping up from near the ground.

The main entrance is to the right and goes into a circular hall, the interior of which carries a winding stairway. This hall opens into the large living room. At the left end of the living room is a huge stone fireplace that might have been lifted from a mountain lodge in the Black Forest.

As the master craftsman of a hundred horror pictures stands beside the fireplace and carefully lights his pipe, your eyes rest on a huge, pillow-piled couch behind him, and you realize it would make a good hiding place for anything, even a body. Then you recall that his latest Monogram picture is *The Corpse Vanishes*, and it seems the air is more chilly than it was.

At the opposite end of the living room is a sprawling piano finished in rough, iron-bound wood harmonizing perfectly with the fireplace. Lugosi touches the keys gracefully, and his large, strong hands seem somehow like those of a surgeon as he plays.

Next to the piano is a huge Dutch door, divided so the top may be opened independently. You step from this doorway into a junglecrowded angle where two tawny beasts stalk toward you, their lips curled back from gleaming fangs.

"Don't move," a voice cautions. Then a word is spoken sternly in Hungarian and the two German shepherds speculatively look to their master as though asking, "What shall be our nourishment today?"

Back in the high-ceilinged living room you notice a balcony above the piano. The effect is weird, for a stream of light from the steeple to the right slashes across it at an angle. You look away for an instant. A board creaks above you and the hair on your neck suddenly seems too short. Then a low voice—Lugosi is standing on the balcony explaining that this is the passageway to the bed chambers, which just now seem unworthy of your investigation.

The dining room opens from the living room. You step through a large, arched doorway into the gloom where a hand-hewn table, flanked by heavy, iron-bound chairs, makes you think of a Gargantuan operating table from the Middle Ages. A wall switch clicks and the scene is flooded with a gentle light·that wipes out the note of a torture chamber.

A long, low hall leads from the dining room, and opening from it is a bar, complete even to cash register. A lantern, the sort you buy if you live far from electric lines, illuminates this replica of a rustic "dive." The blue steel of a grim gun barrel reflects this light and since the barrel is sleek and graceful it seems also to reflect the ominous tone of genteel horror that is the keynote of *Dracula*.

As you walk about the house you are impressed by the almost eerie stillness of the place. Except for a rare squeak of a board that protests your tread, there is no noise. You find you are beginning to feel serene and you almost like the house that horror built.

Then Lugosi remarks with pride, "I love this house. It fits my personality perfectly."

You shiver a bit as you realize all of *Dracula's* victims fell under his spell before he slaughtered them. ■

CROSSWORD PUZZLE SOLUTION

Glide into his Heart

Flower-Fresh the Arthur Murray Way
... USE ODORONO CREAM

● In his arms, gliding to sweet music . . . don't let the magic of the moment escape! Guard your precious appealing freshness the way glamourous Arthur Murray Dancers do—with Odorono Cream! *They* often dance ten miles a day without a moment's fear of disillusioning underarm odor or dampness.

Be glamourous, too! See if gentle Odorono Cream doesn't stop perspiration safely for *you*—up to three whole days at a time! Non-greasy, non-gritty, no waiting to dry. And it will not rot your most fragile frocks. Follow directions. Get a jar—begin today! Generous 10¢, 39¢, 59¢ sizes.

The Odorono Co., Inc., New York

Jean Bjorn,
Nassau teacher, holds partners entranced by her exquisite daintiness.

Stops PERSPIRATION SAFELY 1 TO 3 DAYS

ODO·RO·NO
CREAM DEODORANT
STOPS PERSPIRATION
1 FULL OZ. JAR
—ONLY 39¢
(Plus Tax)

ODORONO CREAM WILL NOT IRRITATE YOUR SKIN

A gathering of Bela's Hungarian friends (far right), which included Victor Varconi (next to Lugosi), Director Michael Curtiz and Paul Lukas (second from right).

Even a man who is pure in heart,
and says his prayers by night,
can become a wolf, when the wolfbane blooms,
and the Autumn moon is bright.
- folklore from
THE WOLF MAN,
by Curt Siodmak

On December 9, 1941, ten years and three days after the release of *Frankenstein*, Universal released *The Wolf Man*. The million-dollar hit boasted the powerhouse cast of Claude Rains, Ralph Bellamy, Warren William, Patric Knowles, Bela Lugosi, Universal's "Queen of Horrors" Evelyn Ankers, and the venerable Maria Ouspenskaya, who quavered the famous prayer:

The way you walked was thorny,
through no fault of your own.
But as the rain enters the soil,
the river enters the sea,
so tears run to their predestined end.
Your suffering is over.
Now you will find peace, for eternity.

Still, there were nightmares in Lugosi's life: the dreadful nature of his Monogram films, like *Spooks Run Wild* (1941), in which he stooged for the Bowery Boys; his supporting player status at Universal, where he had starred as Dracula; the memories of his 1937-1938 unemployment. Always there was the memory of the summer of 1931, when Lugosi scorned the role of the Monster in *Frankenstein*, paving the way for Boris Karloff.

"Bela," Lillian would say, "created his own Monster."

And then, in 1942, Hollywood history wickedly repeated itself.....

Of course, the werewolf over whose corpse Madame Ouspenskaya so fervently prayed was played by Lon Chaney, Jr. (1906-1973). Chaney's classic performance won him Universal's PR accolade as "the new Master Character Creator." The man who truly created the folklore of *The Wolf Man*, however, was writer Curt Siodmak.

Curt Siodmak was Hollywood's top fantasist of the War Years. After success with UFA (Universum Film Aktien Gesselschanft) studios in Germany (where he wrote the screenplay for the 1933 Science Fiction classic, *F.P. 1 Antwortet Nicht*, based on his novel) and Gaumont-British (1935's *Transatlantic Tunnel*), he came to Hollywood in 1937, at the urging of his wife (who feared the horrors of Hitler). His first horror script for Universal was *The Invisible Man Returns* (starring Vincent Price, 1940), followed by the Karloff & Lugosi *Black Friday* (1940), the John Barrymore & Virginia

Curt Siodmak, 1990

UFA Studios, Berlin (Universe Film Company Ltd) - The great German Studio where Siodmak began his career before Hitler and his Nazi party took over Germany. The German film makers who escaped the Nazi terrorism brought their genius to Hollywood in the 30's & 40's.

Bruce *The Invisible Woman* (1941), and, climactically, *The Wolf Man.* Mr. Siodmak himself explained his international survival as a writer:

Story construction - that's why I got paid in every damn country. I could construct a story out of the blue sky. Most writers are dialogue writers, and they produce very worthy dialogue, but there are really very few constructionists who started from scratch. That's why I got jobs.

Less than three weeks after the completion of *The Wolf Man*, Universal rushed *The Ghost of Frankenstein* (1942) into production, with Chaney in the role of the Monster, vacated by Karloff (then performing on Broadway as mad Jonathan Brewster in "Arsenic and Old Lace"). George Waggner (producer/director of *The Wolf Man*) produced, Erle C. Kenton

Lon Chaney Jr. in 1942

directed, and the distinguished cast included Sir Cedric Hardwicke, Ralph Bellamy, Lionel Atwill, Evelyn Ankers, and Bela Lugosi - magnificent in his reprisal of Ygor, the bearded, broken-necked villain from 1939's *Son of Frankenstein.*

In his still-heavy Teutonic accent, Siodmak recently recalled producer George Waggner during an interview at his ranch in the mountains of Three Rivers, California:

My producer at Universal was George Waggner. He was very nice, and he made lots of money for Universal. He was very German in his tastes, and his fun was to drink beer and to sing songs - a typical German-American.

The Ghost of Frankenstein ended with Ygor's brain popped into the Monster's skull, in an evil power plan concocted by Ygor and Atwill's mad Dr. Bohmer; however, the Monster's blood wouldn't feed the sensory nerves in Ygor's brain, and the finale found the Monster roaring (in Ygor's voice) before perishing in the climactic fire. Now, in his revised March 31, 1942 shooting script (included in this book), "Wolf Man Meets Frankenstein," Siodmak afforded juicy dialogue to the Monster (who "officially" had spoken only in Karloff's 1935 *The Bride of Frankenstein*).

Lon Chaney Jr. plays a double header as both Monsters in THE WOLF MAN MEETS FRANKENSTEIN, which goes to bat at Universal this week...
- <u>VARIETY</u>,
October 14, 1942

Over six months would pass between the time Curt Siodmak completed his script, and shooting began. Meanwhile, producer Waggner recruited Roy William Neill (1887 - 1946). Neill had directed Karloff's *The Black Room* (Columbia, 1935) and was then very busy directing Universal's Basil Rathbone/Nigel Bruce *Sherlock Holmes* series.

With Neill, Waggner blueprinted a plan very similar to a formula that Chaney's father had used many times in the silent era: Chaney Jr. would play both the Wolf Man *and* the Monster! Stunt men and doubles could complete the illusion, and "the new Master Character Creator" could enjoy an avalanche of publicity. This concept would last almost to the very eve of shooting. However, Lon Chaney Jr., usually a top professional, could be erratic; he had a terrible life-long problem with alcohol, a violent temper, and impatience with makeup (on the recently-completed *The Mummy's Tomb* Chaney insisted that the rubber mask he wore as "Kharis" gave him an allergy). At the last moment, it was decided Chaney would play only the Wolf Man; after all, as Chaney crowed of the character, "He was my baby!"

Lugosi as Ygor in SON OF FRANKENSTEIN (1939)

Boris Karloff as the original Frankenstein Monster in 1931

So what of the Monster? The most logical candidate was Boris Karloff. Curt Siodmak knew him:

I knew Karloff very well. He came to my house often. He lisped in life - it was funny - and he had a very dark complexion. I don't know what kind of country background he originally had...He was very, very nice - very soft-spoken, and he loved to read children's stories to little boys and girls.

Karloff, however, had vowed respectfully never to play the Monster again after *Son of Frankenstein*; besides, he had just begun a 66-week national tour in "Arsenic and Old Lace." This left Hollywood's only "other" horror name, Bela Lugosi. Says Siodmak:

Bela! I met Bela, of course, but he was a pest. He always called me and said, "Curt! Can you get me zat part? Huh? I want to play zat part!" He had those Hungarian movements. He had created one character - Dracula - and the character had stuck.

Despite Bela's magnificent Ygor in *Son of Frankenstein* and *The Ghost of Frankenstein*, there were powerful men at Universal who shared Siodmak's opinion of Lugosi's talent. One had only to see Lugosi's casting in such roles as the "keeper of the cats" in 1941's *The Black Cat*, the cameo as Bela the gypsy in *The Wolf Man*, and his red herring butler in *Night Monster* to trace his decline in producers' eyes. Still, Bela Lugosi did seem a logical choice for the Monster in *Wolf Man Meets Frankenstein*. With Ygor's brain in the Monster's skull in *The Ghost of Frankenstein*, it seemed almost fitting that Lugosi undertake the part. And he did, after all, have a contract with Universal.

Chaney Jr. as the Monster in GHOST OF FRANKENSTEIN (1942)

However, as Bela had never tired of informing the press, it was he who had turned down the Monster role in 1931, outraged at the prospect of playing a mute "scarecrow." Would he be willing to play the part now?

At this point in his career, Bela Lugosi was willing to play almost anything. As Siodmak states:

Lugosi was glad to get a job again. He was really hard-up. He was already under financial pressure in those days, and there were really few jobs about for him. Karloff did much more.

Lillian Lugosi (who died in 1981) admitted that Siodmak's sentiments were basically true:

Isn't it crazy? After turning down the original, Bela winds up doing it anyhow - THE MONSTER MEETS THE WOLF MAN, or something? He finally did it because of MONEY. He didn't do it any other way!

Bela humbly signed on - but with some definite solace. After all, in this script, the Monster was blind - and spoke! Perhaps Bela justified accepting the role of the monster because he felt it was *now* much more challenging and he enthusiastically eyed Siodmak's dialogue.

Mercifully, he had no idea of the debacle that would follow.

Universal signed the players for "Wolf Man Meets Frankenstein." Top billing, ironically, was awarded to neither monster. That honor was afforded Ilona Massey (1910 - 1974), blonde Hungarian soprano with a true beauty mark, who played Elsa von Frankenstein (the part acted in *The Ghost of Frankenstein* by Evelyn Ankers). The lovely Ilona had arrived in Hollywood in the late 1930s, via the Vienna State Opera, as the pampered protegee of no less than Louis B. Mayer. MGM hailed Ilona as "The Singing Garbo," spending as much as $300 per day for English lessons and vocal training. She scored a great success in 1937's *Rosalie*, the outlandish Cole Porter musical classic with Nelson Eddy and Eleanor Powell, and climaxed her stardom in 1939's *Balalaika*, co-starring with Nelson Eddy. Then, mysteriously, "The Singing Garbo" was dropped by Metro. (According to Hurd Hatfield, who was a personal friend of Miss Massey, the lady had become the mistress of one of Mayer's minion producers; when she ended the relationship, the producer vengefully cancelled her studio contract and tried to blackball her in Hollywood.)

Ilona Massey starred in two 1941 releases for United Artists, *New Wine* and *International Lady*, before signing a two-picture pact with Universal. It wasn't an entirely happy stay. The diva despised playing in 1942's *Invisible Agent*, in which she glamorously stooged for Jon Hall's invisible lead. (According to one source, she was especially aghast at John Fulton's special effect of dangling her in mid-air - supposedly hoisted by Hall - by stringing wires to her corset.) Miss Massey was much happier with *Frankenstein Meets the Wolf Man*.

Ilona Massey and Jon Hall in a production shot from INVISIBLE AGENT (1942).

"Personally, I love horror films," Ilona Massey told reporter James Miller late in her life, "and that's why I did this one. I thought it would be wonderful to do a horror film. I really enjoyed it."

Ilona Massey

§

Patric Knowles and Dennis Hoey listen to Nurse (Doris Lloyd).

Chaney and Lugosi would not even get second-billing in what Universal was heralding as "The Battle of the Century!" Immediately following Ilona in the cast list was Patric Knowles, formerly of Warner Bros., where he played his most famous part (Will Scarlet of 1938's *The Adventures of Robin Hood*) opposite his close crony, Errol Flynn. Having become an all-purpose leading man at Universal (where, incidentally, he played Evelyn Ankers' fiance in *The Wolf Man*), Knowles was well-cast as Dr. Frank Mannering (called "Dr. Harley" in Siodmak's original), being a fine enough actor to sound sincere when he cries, "I can't destroy Frankenstein's creation! I've got to see it at its full power!"; and handsome enough to give Ilona somebody to cling to in the final reel.

"I was under contract to Universal," the genial Mr. Knowles recently recalled in an interview with <u>The World of Bela Lugosi</u>, the newsletter of the now unfortunately-defunct Lugosi fan club, "and I did what I was told!"

Universal appeased Chaney with special "And" billing in the credits. However, in the opening credits*, Bela Lugosi

Lionel Atwill as the Mayor of Vasaria

had to settle for billing below yet another actor - Lionel Atwill. The British star on such classics as Warners' 1932 *Doctor X* and 1933 *Mystery of the Wax Museum*, as well as the one-armed Inspector Krogh of Universal's *Son of Frankenstein* and mad Dr. Bohmer of *The Ghost of Frankenstein*, had just provided Basil Rathbone with a marvelous Professor Moriarty (Holmes' arch-rival in Conan Doyle's detective stories) in *Sherlock Holmes and the Secret Weapon*. Atwill took the part of the jolly Mayor of Vasaria - and was grateful for it; he was in the tempest of a courtroom melodrama dealing with his private life.

On October 15, 1942, three days after *Frankenstein Meets the Wolf Man* began shooting, Atwill was sentenced to five years' probation for perjury, and the shocked Hays Office issued a mandate in Hollywood not to hire the actor. Rumor circulated that Universal would fire Atwill after his sentencing, but they stood behind their veteran star and he remained on *Frankenstein Meets the Wolf Man*.

"But for the courage and magnanimity of one particular studio," said Atwill later of Universal, "I guess I should be a dead egg now."

Maria Ouspenskaya

Universal nicely stocked the supporting cast. Grand, 66-year old Maria Ouspenskaya ("a nice little old lady with a steel spine," remembers Patric Knowles), of the Russian Art Theatre, reprised her role of Maleva, the gypsy seer of *The Wolf Man*.

*In a compromise, Universal billed Atwill first on the opening credits, but Lugosi first on posters and lobby cards.

*Rex Evans holds Wolf Man victim Martha MacVicar
(Dwight Frye far right, Adia Kuznetzoff holds lantern).*

Dennis Hoey, then winning popularity as Scotland Yard's thick-skulled Lestrade of the *Sherlock Holmes* series, was in his blustery element as Inspector Owen. Stout Rex Evans, memorable as Katharine Hepburn's butler of MGM's *The Philadelphia Story* (1940), enjoyed the role of Vazec, the raving innkeeper. Poor Dwight Frye, today revered for his roles as "fly-eater" Renfield of *Dracula*, hunchbacked dwarf Fritz of *Frankenstein*, and grave-robbing Karl of *The Bride of Frankenstein*, made his fifth appearance in a Frankenstein film as Rudi, a nervous villager who (in the script, but not noted in the release print) was a newlywed. (So perilous was Frye's fortune at this time that he worked as a tool designer at the Douglas Aircraft Plant on the night shift, hunting movie jobs by day.)

Adia Kuznetzoff, the Russian bass of gypsy roots who rolled his eyes and operatic tones in several Hollywood films, was cast as the Festival Singer, who belts out the famous "Faro-la, faro-li" song. And Martha MacVicar, who later became Martha Vickers, Warner star of the late '40s (and the third Mrs. Mickey Rooney), made her film bow as Margareta, the lifeless victim of the Wolf Man during his first evening in Vasaria.

Dwight Frye - a pre-Hollywood, Broadway portrait (1927)

Cast assembled, George Robinson at the camera, Vera West supplying Miss Massey with stunning costumes, John P. Fulton and David Horsley supervising Special Effects, Jack P. Pierce ruling the makeup roost, and a budget in the neighborhood of $300,000, *Wolf Man Meets Frankenstein* began shooting under pleasant conditions on Monday, October 12, 1942.

Chaney reacts to Curt Siodmak's lyrics "For life is short, but death is long, Faro-la-Faro-li." (Music by Hans J. Salter)

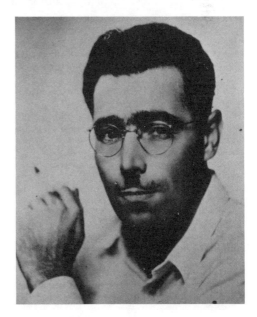

Special Effects genius David S. Horsley

19

The Festival of the New Wine

Producer Waggner ordered splendid sets for the film. Set Decorator Russell Gausman provided the proper Bavarian atmosphere on the back lot village for the Festival of the New Wine, in which 500 extras celebrated; he also decorated Universal's *Phantom* Stage, where certain scenes for that sequence were shot on the soundstage set. The old graveyard set never looked more bleak and foreboding than it did for the opening desecration of the Talbot mausoleum. Ilona Massey, in the words of Patric Knowles, was "a joy to look at and work with," and Lon Chaney, generally on his best behavior, charmed his leading lady, who recalled: *I think Lon Chaney is one of the nicest, sweetest people in the world. It was a great deal of fun. You know it took four hours to put on his makeup and when it was on, it was hot under the lights. It was very difficult for him to eat. He mostly had soup which he sipped through a straw and just for fun, we put hot peppers in it! We had a lot of fun...I never had any difficulty with my co-stars, but Chaney was something special.*

Ilona Massey with Nelson Eddy in BALALAIKA (MGM).

Lon's "best pal" Moose poses with Illona Massey.

20

Chaney was delighted when Moose, the German Shepherd who was his constant companion on the Universal lot, landed a part in *Frankenstein Meets the Wolf Man*: Bruno, the barking dog in the gypsy camp. (Moose even gets a nice close-up!) At the time, the 36-year old Chaney (according to Louella Parsons) was "moving heaven and earth" to try to enlist in the Marines as a cook. Shortly after *Frankenstein Meets the Wolf Man* he did enter the Army, but quickly was reclassified 4-F and returned to Universal.

Bruno the Gypsy Dog

John P. Fulton, Universal's Special Effects maestro, perfected the famed metamorphosis, and for the first time, Chaney's Talbot changed from man to wolf before the audience's eyes (he had only reverted from wolf to man in *The Wolf Man*).

John P. Fulton, pioneer of modern movie special effects

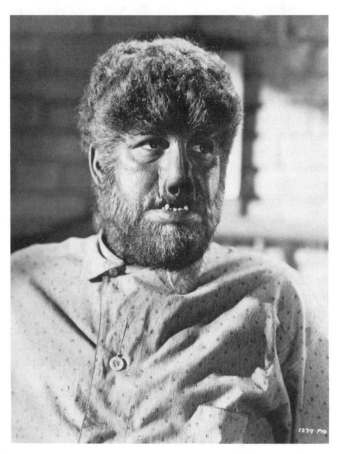

21

Chaney vividly remembered the ordeal:

The day we did the transformations I came in at 2:00 a.m. When I hit that position they would take little nails and drive them through the skin at the end of my fingers, on both hands, so that I wouldn't move them anymore...

The crew then built a plaster cast of the back of Chaney's head, starched the drapes behind him, weighed the camera down with a one ton weight so it wouldn't quiver, set targets for Chaney's eyes, and shot five or ten frames of film. Then Jack Pierce would put a new makeup on the still-pinned and immobile Chaney. Then another five or ten frames would be shot, the makeup changed again. As Chaney later grunted:

...We did 21 changes of makeup and it took 22 hours. I won't discuss about the bathroom!

Chaney could take it, he was only 36 years old. Bela Lugosi, in the midst of shooting on October 20, 1942, turned 60.

"A quiet and lonely man...seemed unhappy," recalled Patric Knowles of Bela Lugosi. Although Bela was living in his lovely Whipple Street house at the time, very close to Universal, his wife Lillian still remembered the engagement as a terrible strain:

I, of course, drove Bela to work (he never did learn to drive; my father offered to teach him how once and Bela said, "No, I want Lillian to drive me where I want to go"). Anyway, when he played the Monster, he had to be at the studio at 5 o'clock in the morning. That headpiece weighed 5 pounds; those boots together weighed over 20 pounds; the whole schmeer took like four hours to get on. They had a special chair on the set for the Monster to sit in...

Sadly, it was quickly obvious to all that Lugosi's casting as the Monster was a grievous mistake. First of all, Jack Pierce's beauty clay couldn't dominate Bela's patrician nose, dimpled chin and noble features; a new, smaller, specially designed forehead piece (molded by Ellis Burman Sr., who made Universal's rubber makeup pieces) didn't help. Secondly, Lugosi's health was failing, and he simply couldn't tolerate the mercilessly heavy costume, four-hour makeup torture each morning, and 15- to 16-hour workdays. The very professional Bela did all he could to rise to the occasion, even getting up at 2:30 a.m. to soak in a hot tub to prepare himself for each day's challenge. Still, it was painfully clear that the actor could never play the more demanding scenes of the script, especially the climactic fight with the Wolf Man.

Finally, Waggner and Neill decided that emergency action must be taken. It was too late to remove Lugosi without embarrassing repercussions for the actor and the studio. So what to do?

The panacea for the sensitive production ailment arrived in the six-foot-four form of Eddie Parker, 41-year old Hollywood stunt man and bit player, then busy at Universal. A few months earlier, the strapping Parker had won a special niche in action cinema by taking the nastier knocks in the classic John Wayne/Randolph Scott slugfest in Universal's *The Spoilers*. More relevantly, Parker had doubled for Chaney, both as the Monster in *The Ghost of Frankenstein* and Kharis in *The Mummy's Ghost*. Waggner and Neill recruited Parker, unbilled and sworn to secrecy, to don the Monster guise (busy days for Jack Pierce!) and lurk in the soundstage shadows, prepared to step before the camera whenever Bela was overwhelmed. Ironically, Parker, with his great neck muscles, looked much more impressive in the Monster makeup than did Lugosi - so much so that Neill used Parker in the opening shot of the ice-bound Monster, bolstering the audience's first impression of the creature! (This was fine with Bela, who hardly cherished the thought of cramming his aching body behind the wall of ice.)

Stuntman Eddie Parker doubling for Lugosi

As Bela sat in the special "Monster Chair," puffing a cigar as he watched Parker perform the more strenuous action, he was a bit embarrassed by his situation - though not much more than he was by the part itself. Once, after unleashing a fearsome growl when Massey, Knowles and Ouspenskaya approached the Frankenstein ruins, Lugosi abashedly turned to Neill, shook his head, and smiled.

That YELL is the worst thing about the part, grimaced Lugosi. *You feel like a big jerk every time you do it!*

Even with the trials of portraying the Monster, Lugosi gallantly was organizing the American Hungarian Defense Federation in Los Angeles during his stint as Frankenstein's Monster. The 10,000 Los Angeles Hungarians managed to donate $1,600 to the Red Cross, buy $65,000 in War Bonds in one day, and completely equip an ambulance for overseas action.

§

Lugosi campaigning with the Hungarian Defense Federation

assignment of scoring the film, and rarely did he perform so nobly. In an interview with Preston Neal Jones in <u>Cinefantastique</u> (Summer 1978), Salter recalled:

In those days, we had no idea we were writing for "eternity." We were just trying to keep up the frantic pace of picture after picture. Let's say it was Monday - the producer showed you his picture. You had to write a score, and orchestrate it, and be ready to rehearse and record with the orchestra the following Monday. It was like a factory, where you'd have to produce a certain amount of red socks, a certain amount of green socks....

Salter created some chilling musical effects, reprising themes from the milestone score that he, Charles Previn and Frank Skinner had written for 1941's *The Wolf Man*. A special highlight is the now famous "Faro-la, faro-li" song (with lyrics by Curt Siodmak), sung at the Festival of the New Wine*:

> Come one and all and sing a song,
> Faro-la, faro-li!
> For life is short but death is long,
> Faro-la, faro-li!

Adia Kuznetzoff, who sang the song, was (as Salter remembers) *"a very pleasant fellow. He was a Russian Gypsy by heritage, and when we prerecorded this song he just ate it up. He loved doing it."*

In the Spring of 1977, when Salter was honored by the University of California at Los Angeles Extension and the Los Angeles Film Exposition in a program devoted to Fantasy, Horror and Science Fiction, the first reel of *Frankenstein Meets the Wolf Man* was shown to exemplify the artistry of Salter.

Editing was not so fortunate.

There came the inevitable day when Waggner, Neill, Siodmak, and various members of the production staff of *Frankenstein Meets the Wolf Man* congregated in a studio screening room to see the finished product. All were enjoying Neill's superbly atmospheric direction, Chaney's powerful star performance and Ilona Massey's beauty - until there came the scene which originally followed Talbot's rescuing the Monster from the ice. The two nightmares shared a fire in the ruins, and had a conversation.

The audience in the screening room was almost in hysterics. Curt Siodmak explains:

Do you know why they took the Monster's dialogue away? Because Bela Lugosi couldn't talk! They had left the dialogue I wrote for the Monster in the picture when they shot it, but with Lugosi it sounded so Hungarian funny that they had to take it out! Seriously!

Lugosi was good as Dracula, because it supplied him with a Hungarian part. But a MONSTER with a HUNGARIAN accent?!

Universal's Frankenstein sagas were all cursed by accidents - and *Frankenstein Meets the Wolf Man* proved no exception. On Thursday, November 5, 1942, Maria Ouspenskaya was rushed to Cedars of Lebanon Hospital; <u>The Hollywood Reporter</u> noted that a carriage had run over her foot, fracturing her ankle. <u>Photoplay</u> magazine gave a much more colorful account: *"It seems the pair were riding in a heavy iron cart through a wooded path on the set of FRANKENSTEIN MEETS THE WOLF MAN, when suddenly the cart overturned, pinning them both underneath. Had the horse bolted, the accident would have had unthinkable consequences. Instead, he stood still midst the cries and confusion until Lon and Madame could be extracted. Madame's leg was fractured. Lon suffered severe cuts."* At any rate, Madame Ouspenskaya left Cedars on November 9, while Chaney, reportedly, loyally visited the horse at its back lot stable to rub its head affectionately.

And, on November 5, there was another accident: Bela Lugosi collapsed on the set. A physician diagnosed his condition as exhaustion, ordered the actor home and blamed the collapse on Bela's 35-lb. Monster get-up.

TITANS OF TERROR! Clashing in Mortal Combat!
- Universal promotional copy for
Frankenstein Meets the Wolf Man

On Wednesday, November 11, 1942 (Patric Knowles' birthday), *Frankenstein Meets the Wolf Man* completed shooting. A relieved Bela removed the Monster makeup, boots and costume for the last time, and post-production began in the areas of musical score and editing. Hans Salter drew the

---

* As will be seen in the shooting script, the song originally had verses not heard in the film, including comic verses sung to drunk Don Barclay and newlywed Dwight Frye.

For the audience in the screening room, the "topper" came in a scene at the Frankenstein ruins, after the Monster had crashed the Festival of the New Wine.

LARRY
Why did you come down to the village?
Now they'll hunt us again -

MONSTER:
I was afraid you'd left me -
I thought you'd found that diary - and run away -

LARRY(bitterly):
You think you're so clever
- Frankenstein gave you a cunning brain, did he?
But you're dumb! You've spoiled our only chance -

MONSTER
(as the Doctor's voice is heard calling Talbot):
Don't leave me - don't go! I'm weak..They'll
catch me and bury me alive!...

That did it. With Lugosi delivering his Monster dialogue as fervently as he had played Romeo on the Hungarian stage, producer Waggner was terrified that "the beast battle of the century" would reap laughs. Desperately, he ordered Editor Edward Curtiss to cut all of the Monster's dialogue. Out came the scene by the fire, and the "I was afraid.." vignette, as well as the Monster's musings before the climactic operation. In the sequence where Talbot discovers the portrait of Elsa Frankenstein, and is told by the Monster who she is, the Monster's dialogue was simply erased from the soundtrack - poor Lugosi stands there, his mouth flapping mutely! Along with the deleted dialogue, all references to the Monster's blindness were expunged as well. Hence, Lugosi's stretching and groping mannerisms no longer made any sense. Ironically, these Lugosi mannerisms have been remembered throughout the decades, and whenever the Frankenstein Monster is imitated by children it is always with outstretched arms and blindly stumbling about.

The damage done to Bela Lugosi's sincere but weak performance was devastating*.

New York's Universal Horror Theater - The Rialto, where many of the Universal classic horror films had their debut.
FRANKENSTEIN MEETS THE WOLF MAN was received with the same enthusiasm in 1943.

*In the late 1980s, when MCA Video restored the original *Dracula* and *Frankenstein*, a search was made for the edited footage from *Frankenstein Meets the Wolf Man*. As Michael Fitzgerald, Vice President of MCA Video related, ...we tried to find original nitrate tracks of Chaney and Lugosi walking and talking and babbling on and on - obviously, you can see Lugosi's Monster's mouth moving in the film. So far, the footage has not been found.

Universal's *Frankenstein Meets the Wolf Man*, with its emergency editing, previewed in Los Angeles February 18, 1943. Variety was impressed: *Here's a strong dish for the mass of customers who go for the bizarre, the weird, the creepy...*

...Picture, cannily produced by George Waggner and skillfully directed by Roy William Neill, also benefits from excellent performances by Chaney, Lugosi, Patric Knowles, as a doctor, Maria Ouspenskaya, a Gypsy ....

Spectacular and sensational effects are properly emphasized in the script by Curtis Siodmak and in the fine camerawork by George Robinson.....

Variety's only complaint was the "spotty performance" of Miss Massey. "She is permitted to be too casual in a number of scenes which should have been dominated by more reactionary terror." Nevertheless, Universal sighed in relief: the press audience hadn't noted the editing.

The Hollywood Reporter gave a show business perspective: *Roosevelt meets Churchill at Casablanca, Yanks meet Japs at Guadalcanal - and yet these events will fade into insignificance to those seemingly inexhaustible legions of horror fans when they hear that FRANKENSTEIN MEETS THE WOLF MAN. Yay, brother!...*

Frankenstein Meets the Wolf Man opened at New York City's Rialto Theatre March 5, 1943. Universal offered exhibitors a carnival of audience-luring techniques. In the February issue of major magazines, a Max Factor makeup advertisement featured a beautiful portrait of Ilona Massey and a "plug" for *Frankenstein Meets the Wolf Man*. The pressbook offered schemes to stir local interest - including a "Where would the Wolf Man and Frankenstein hide in your town?" contest, calling for essays and photographs. *Frankenstein Meets the Wolf Man* led off the 1943 horror output for Universal, followed by such thrillers as *Captive Wild Woman* (introducing Acquanetta as "Paula the Ape Woman"), *The Mad Ghoul* (with George Zucco, Evelyn Ankers, and David Bruce in the withered title role), *Son of Dracula* (featuring Lon Chaney as Count Alucard - spell it backward!) and, of course, the Technicolor *Phantom of the Opera*. All contributed solidly to the studio's walloping $3.8 million fiscal profit for 1943.

There were several professional and personal repercussions in the wake of *Frankenstein Meets the Wolf Man*.

Curt Siodmak's classic novel Donovan's Brain was published in 1943, consolidating the writer as a major fantasy author. (There have been many film versions.)

Ilona Massey, free of her Universal bonds, temporarily fled Hollywood for Broadway. On April 1, 1943, she opened in a new edition of "Ziegfeld Follies," co-starring with Milton Berle and Arthur Treacher. The lavish revue presented Ilona with stunning costumes and lovely songs, and ran for 553 performances. (After a mixed bag career of films, television and concerts, Miss Massey retired after 1960; she died August 20, 1974, at the Naval Hospital in Bethesda, MD.)

25

Lionel Atwill appealed his perjury conviction, and was exonerated in April, 1943. He returned to work as "the Scarab" in Republic's 1944 *Captain America* serial; played featured roles in such films as Universal's *House of Frankenstein* (1944) and *House of Dracula* (1945); and wed (for the fourth time) in 1944, his bride a young radio producer/singer named Paula Pruter. On October 14, 1945, the 60-year old Atwill became the father of Lionel Atwill Jr. Atwill was at work as the villain of Universal's 1946 serial *Lost City of the Jungle* when he became ill with bronchial cancer; the studio finished the serial with a double. Lionel Atwill died at his Pacific Palisades house on April 22, 1946. He was 61 years old.

Maria Ouspenskaya died December 3, 1949, of a stroke and burns suffered as a result of smoking in bed. She was 73 years old.

Tragically, *Frankenstein Meets the Wolf Man* would prove to be the final Frankenstein saga for the peaked Dwight Frye. In order to support his wife and son, contribute to the war effort, and maintain his home at 2590 N. Beachwood Drive in the Hollywood Hills, Frye had been designing bombsights on the night shift at the Douglas Aircraft plant. By day, he haunted the casting offices. In November of 1943, Frye was thrilled to land the small but dynamic part of Newton D. Baker, Secretary of War, in 20th Century-Fox's projected epic, *Wilson*. The last night of his life - Sunday, November 7, 1943 - Frye celebrated by taking his wife Laura and 12-year old Dwight Jr. to the movies. As Dwight Frye Jr. told John Antosiewicz and Charlie Rizzo in an interview in <u>Midnight Marquee</u> magazine:

...I remember the three of us went to see a movie at the Pantages Theatre on Hollywood and Vine. I don't recall what the movie was but do remember our having to wait in line in this rather warm theatre for a long time. We got in to see the movie, it was crowded, came out of the movie and we ran to the corner to catch the bus to go home. As we got on the bus and it pulled away my father dropped in the middle of the aisle of the bus....

Dwight Frye died of a heart attack late that night at Hollywood Receiving Hospital. He was 44. The little actor, once a Broadway star, today revered for his roles in *Dracula*, *Frankenstein*, and *The Bride of Frankenstein*, was identified on his death certificate as a "Tool Designer."

Eddie Parker kept busy in features and serials; at Universal he went on to double Karloff in *Abbott and Costello Meet Dr. Jekyll and Mr. Hyde* (1953), and play one of the Metaluna Mutants in *This Island Earth*, the Mummy in *Abbott and Costello Meet the Mummy*, and a disfigured scientist in *Tarantula* - all 1955 releases. Ironically, he reportedly doubled a sadly frail Bela Lugosi as the mad scientist of Banner's 1956 release, *Bride of the Monster*. Eddie Parker died of a heart attack at his Sherman Oaks home on January 20, 1960.

Patric Knowles is still active today, and volunteers his time at the Motion Picture Home in Woodland Hills, teaching crafts. In fact, he used to visit George Waggner, producer of *Frankenstein Meets the Wolf Man*, before Waggner's death in 1984.

Lon Chaney went on to enjoy a very active career as both a horror star and a character actor, eventually playing in over 150 feature films and scores of television shows. After bravely battling many illnesses (including throat cancer, which had killed Lon Chaney, Sr. in 1930), he died of a heart attack in San Clemente, California on July 12, 1973. He was 67 years old. *"They don't know how to make good horror films in Hollywood anymore,"* said Chaney shortly before his death. *"Boy, they really need me!"*

And as for Bela Lugosi....*Frankenstein Meets the Wolf Man* completed his stay at Universal. He would return to the lot once more, for Universal-International's *Abbott and Costello Meet Frankenstein* (1948). Hollywood apathy, a divorce from Lillian in 1953, and, so tragically, drug addiction, stemming from a 1944 medical accident, could have made his last years very sad ones. In April, 1955, the actor committed himself as a drug addict to Metropolitan State Hospital. He was released in the minimum amount of time - 3 months - leaving the hospital a cured but frail man. He married a middle-aged fan, Hope Lininger, in August, 1955, and longed for a comeback. However, the only roles he found were as a mute servant in *The Black Sleep* (1956) and the "Ghoul Man" in Edward D. Wood's notorious *Plan 9 From Outer Space*, released in 1959. There was an irony in both these roles for the star who had originally scorned *Frankenstein* for its lack of dialogue, and had his dialogue in *Frankenstein Meets the Wolf Man* deleted: both parts were mute.*

[We will always hold great admiration for the monumental courage of the great Hungarian actor to admit to the world his drug addiction, especially in the social climate of the 50's. But when he overcame its deadly grip at the age of 73, he unknowingly became an inspiration to many with the same problem over the decades that followed - a legacy even greater than his long film and stage career. - Ed.]

Bela Lugosi died of a heart attack at his apartment, 5620 Harold Way in Hollywood, on August 16, 1956. According to his final wishes, the star was buried at Holy Cross Cemetery in his Dracula cape.

———————

Oh, with all that makeup on it's impossible for anyone to tell it isn't me. Every time they make another Frankenstein picture, I get all the fan mail. The other fellow gets the check!
- Boris Karloff

Frankenstein Meets the Wolf Man has long reigned as one of Universal's most popular Horror classics. The sure, sound atmospheric direction of Roy William Neill is most impres-

---

*Lugosi was also originally cast as The Wolf Man in a 1939-40 story originally written for Karloff in 1932 by Robert Florey - the scheduled director was Erle C. Kenton who had directed Lugosi in *The Island of Lost Souls* (based on H.G. Wells' <u>Island of Dr. Moreau</u>) for Paramount in 1932. Lugosi portrayed "The sayer of the law," half-man, half-wolf. When Chaney signed with Universal, a totally new and original script was conceived by Curt Siodmak. - Ed.

sive, especially his staging of the "Festival of the New Wine" episode, which gives the movie a touch of the Grimms' fairy tale quality with which James Whale garnished the first two *Frankenstein* adventures. The special effects of John P. Fulton and the musical score of Hans J. Salter are of inestimable assistance, while the climactic, 110-second fight between the Monster and the Wolf Man remains an exciting horror film event.

Ilona Massey, a great beauty, brings a touch of MGM class to the melodrama, while Patric Knowles strikes a comfortable balance between horror film hero and determined scientist. Lionel Atwill's Burgomaster has the proper Tyrolean touch (he reveals himself quite the dancer as he twirls the beaming Miss Massey about in a spirited folk dance at the Festival!), while Maria Ouspenskaya's Maleva is choked with Stanislavskian fervor.

Of course, it is Lon Chaney who really carries *Frankenstein Meets the Wolf Man*, creating and sustaining a pathos that conveys the tragedy, and not just the melodrama, of the lycanthropic Talbot.

Then there's Bela Lugosi. Unfortunately, his performance of Frankenstein's Monster is the most maligned, panned and roasted performance of Universal's horror shows. Actually, his performance does have its moments, such as the evil smile that flickers as Knowles restores him to full power (and, as originally shot, to full sight). Indeed, after watching Lugosi's performance (and learning of the behind-the-scenes mayhem), one does not feel scorn for the performance as much as pity for the actor.

Nevertheless, in spite of the problems (and perhaps because of them), Lugosi's Frankenstein Monster has become a classic in itself. When MCA/Universal Home Video released *Frankenstein Meets the Wolf Man* on video cassette in the fall of 1986, all New York shops virtually sold out the cassette on the very first day of its release.

■■■■■■■■■■■■■■■■■■■■■■■

[*Frankenstein Meets the Wolf Man* marked the end of the Frankenstein family members appearing in the Universal classics: Henry Frankenstein, portrayed by Colin Clive in *Frankenstein* (1931) and *The Bride of Frankenstein* (1935); his wife Elizabeth, portrayed by Mae Clarke in *Frankenstein* and Valerie Hobson in *The Bride of Frankenstein*; their son Wolf and his wife Elsa, portrayed by Basil Rathbone and Josephine Hutchinson in *Son of Frankenstein* (1939); Wolf's brother Ludwig, portrayed by Sir Cedric Hardwicke in *The Ghost of Frankenstein* (1942); and Ludwig's daughter Elsa, portrayed by Ilona Massey in *Frankenstein Meets the Wolf Man* (1943). In the last three films - *House of Frankenstein* (1944), *House of Dracula* (1945) and *Abbott and Costello Meet Frankenstein* (1948) - only the Monster bearing the Frankenstein name appeared. - Ed.]

FRANKENSTEIN MEETS THE WOLF MAN

STUDIO: Universal
PRODUCER: George Waggner
DIRECTOR: Roy William Neill
ORIGINAL SCREENPLAY: Curtis Siodmak
DIRECTOR OF PHOTOGRAPHY: George Robinson
ART DIRECTOR: John B. Goodman
ASSOCIATE ART DIRECTION: Martin Obzina,
SOUND: Bernard B. Brown (William Fox, Technician)
SET DECORATIONS: Russell A. Gausman
                E.R. Robinson, (Associate)
FILM EDITOR: Edward Curtiss
GOWNS: Vera West
MUSICAL DIRECTOR: Hans J. Salter
ASSISTANT DIRECTOR: Melville Shyer
SPECIAL PHOTOGRAPHIC EFFECTS: John P. Fulton
                (David S. Horsley, Associate)
MAKEUP ARTIST: Jack P. Pierce

Running Time: 74 minutes

THE PLAYERS

Baroness Elsa Frankenstein	Ilona Massey
Dr. Frank Mannering	Patric Knowles
The Mayor	Lionel Atwill
The Monster	Bela Lugosi
Maleva	Maria Ouspenskaya
Inspector Owen	Dennis Hoey
Franzec	Don Barclay
Vazec	Rex Evans
Rudi	Dwight Frye
Cuno	Harry Stubbs
and	
Lawrence Talbot, The Wolf Man	Lon Chaney
with	
The Festival Singer	Adia Kuznetzoff
Erno	Torben Meyer
The Constable	Charles Irwin
The Nurse	Doris Lloyd
The Grave Robbers	Tom Stevenson
	Cyril Delevanti
The Sergeant	David Clyde
Grave Digger	Jeff Corey
Rudi's Wife	Beatrice Roberts
Margareta, Village Girl	Martha MacVicar*
Bruno (dog in gypsy camp)	Moose
Double for Lugosi	Eddie Parker

Filmed at Universal City, California, 12 October - 11 November, 1942; premiere, the Rialto Theatre, New York City, March 5, 1943.

Available on MCA/Universal Videocasette and Laser-Disc.

---

* Later known as Martha Vickers.

Luck
Lon Chaney

Lon Chaney Jr.

Bela Lugosi

Ilona Massey

Ilona Massey

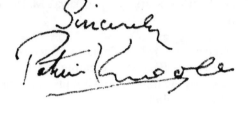

Patric Knowles

Lionel Atwill '31

Lionel Atwill

Curt Siodmak

Curt Siodmak

Hans J. Salter

Hans J. Salter

28

Behind the Scenes

Lon and Moose became best friends

Illona Massey breaks up during a photo session as Moose breaks into the shot.

29

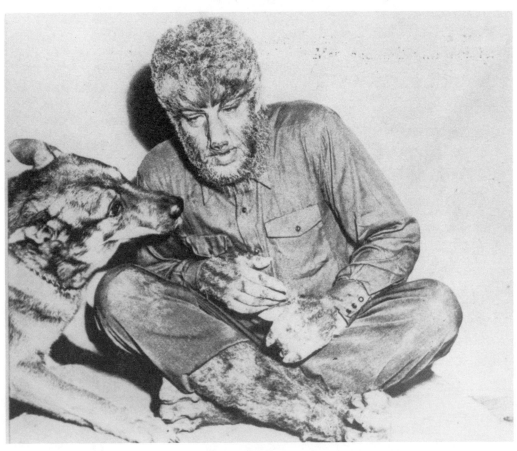

30

(Above) Bela Jr. visits his proud father
(Below) Ilona Massey studying her script

31

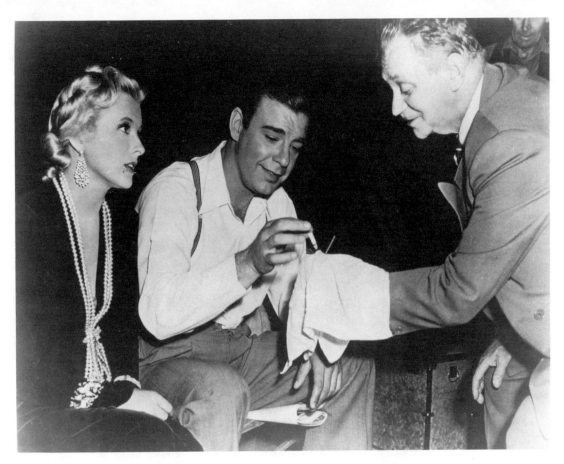

(Above) Ilona Massey and Lon take part in a magic trick.
(Below) Back to work as Jack Pierce prepares Chaney for a publicity photo.

(Above) Chaney holds up under the hours of Wolf Man makeup application by Pierce.
(Below) Pierce's red-hot singeing iron puts the final touches on Chaney, who looks none too pleased about the smell.

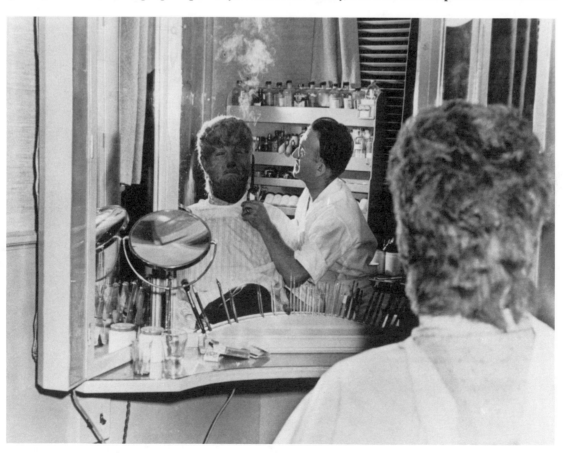

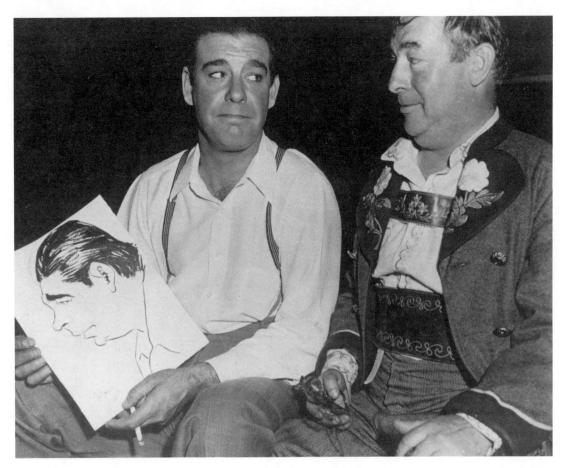

Extra and caricaturist Don Barclay entertains the stars during breaks. Chaney Jr. was so proud of his sketch that he kept it for use in his book A Century of Chaneys. Even Shemp Howard got the caricature treatment from Barclay when he visited the set.

34

(Above) The Miniature Castle destroyed by the flood at the end of the film.
(Below) Three stunt doubles take over for Ilona Massey, Patric Knowles and Chaney for the climactic lab explosions.

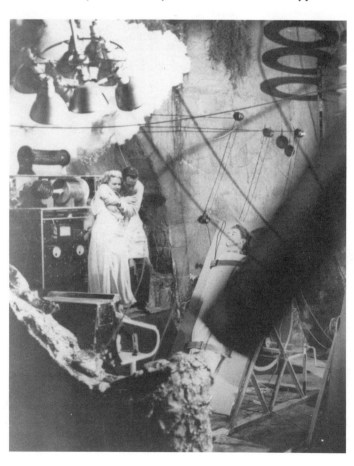

(Above) Lugosi expresses the blindness of the Monster in this publicity photo.

(Below) Bela shines through his torment giving us just a hint of what his part could have been.

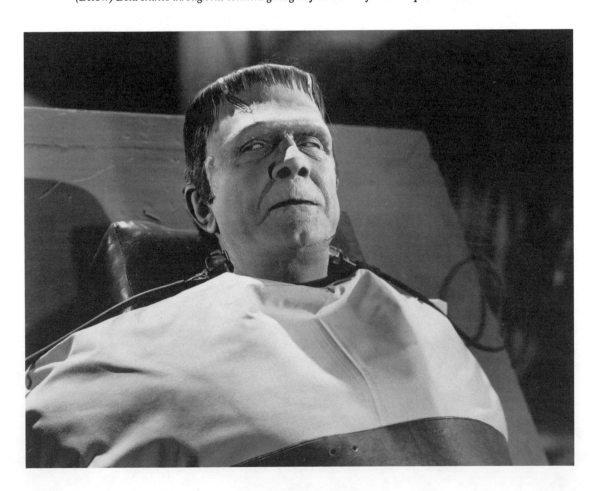

(Above) Lugosi's age shows even behind the heavy makeup.
(Below) Chaney strikes a classic pose in his second time around as the Wolf Man

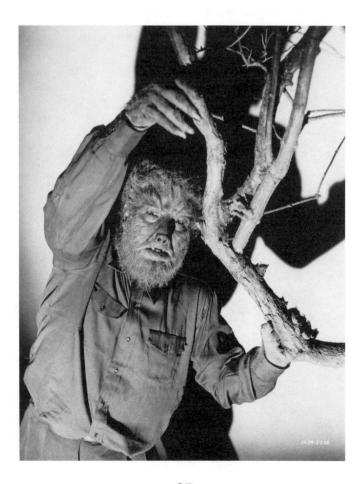

Six scenes which involved the Monster's dialogue as you will read in the script (pages 63-69 & 112-114). The whole concept of Lugosi as a speaking Frankenstein Monster makes complete sense, having Ygor's brain transplanted into its skull at the end of the last feature - and his voice carried well, although not matching well with Chaney Jr's facial expressions. When THE GHOST OF FRANKENSTEIN is released on MCA/Universal Home Video you will have the chance to hear Lugosi's voice as the Monster, giving new life to Curt Siodmak's dialogue, which would have worked with Ygor's raspy broken-necked rattle.

MONSTER: Where are you? I can hardly see . .
LARRY: Watch out you'll burn yourself . . .
MONSTER: Burn myself? . .Help me get up . What are you doing here?

LARRY: Hiding. . . the same as you
MONSTER: Those futile little mortals! Do you hate them, too?
LARRY: Yes...How do we get out of here?

MONSTER:The laboratory must be behind the ice - No up here! I remember now.
      If Dr. Frankenstein were still alive he would restore my sight...restore my strength so that I could live forever.
LARRY: Don't you want to die?.....Where is that diary?

(Above) MONSTER: The story of my creation is written in Dr. Frankenstein's diary. He knew the secret of immortality - and he knew the secret of death!

(Below) MONSTER: The ice is melting...The machines will work again - and the Doctor will make me strong once more. [Maleva enters scene with some food - the Monster retreats to the cave wall.]

LARRY (to Maleva) I can feel the spell beginning...

Music

*Following are Hans J. Salter's cover sheets for three of the brilliant themes he created
(which played the most important part in saving the film from falling into the "B" category).*

First Transformation

by H.J. Salter

Hans J. Salter with Deanna Durbin in a Universal projection room, circa 1942.

Exterior Sets

Two angles showing the village where the Wolf Man and Maleva stop to inquire about Dr. Frankenstein

This set also appeared, although it was more prominent in THE GHOST OF FRANKENSTEIN; where Chaney, as the Monster,
went up to retrieve the little girl's balloon and later tossed it down on a few of the villagers.
Some of these sets still exist and can be seen as on the Universal City Tour.

(Above) The Wolf Man escapes from the hospital and seeks his first victim, a policeman on his nightly security check. (Below) Trying to escape the villagers, Talbot falls into the ice caverns where he discovers the frozen Monster.

The opening scene where the two grave robbers unknowingly revive the Wolf Man by removing the wolfbane from his coffin.

The police find the body of one of the unfortunate grave robbers.

Larry Talbot and Maleva discover that Dr. Frankenstein is dead.

Having tracked down Elsa Frankenstein, Talbot, Maleva and Dr. Mannering go to the ruins of the Frankenstein Castle and discover Talbot's hiding place for the monster.

*In search of his new friend, Talbot, the Monster
wanders into the village during the festival.*

Talbot attempts to escape with the Monster.

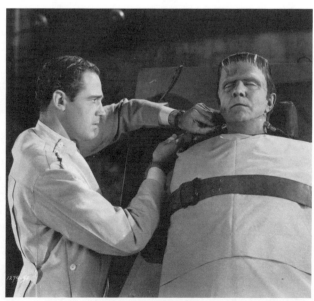

Dr. Mannering falls under the scientific spell of the Frankensteins and begins to revive the Monster instead of destroying it.

A recent remarkable find by the Art Directors of Universal Orlando Studios - the life masks of Lon Chaney Jr., Bela Lugosi, Boris Karloff, Lou Costello and other stars. These molds, with the exception of Jack Pierce's headpiece for Lugosi and Chaney's face used for his Mummy mask in the MUMMY sequels, were used by Bud Westmore and Jack Kevan for the later films. These, and other artifacts, can be seen at THE PHANTOM OF THE OPERA MAKEUP SHOW- Universal Studios Florida in Orlando.

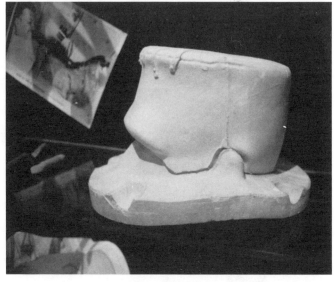

Glenn Strange's "Frankenstein" headpiece

49

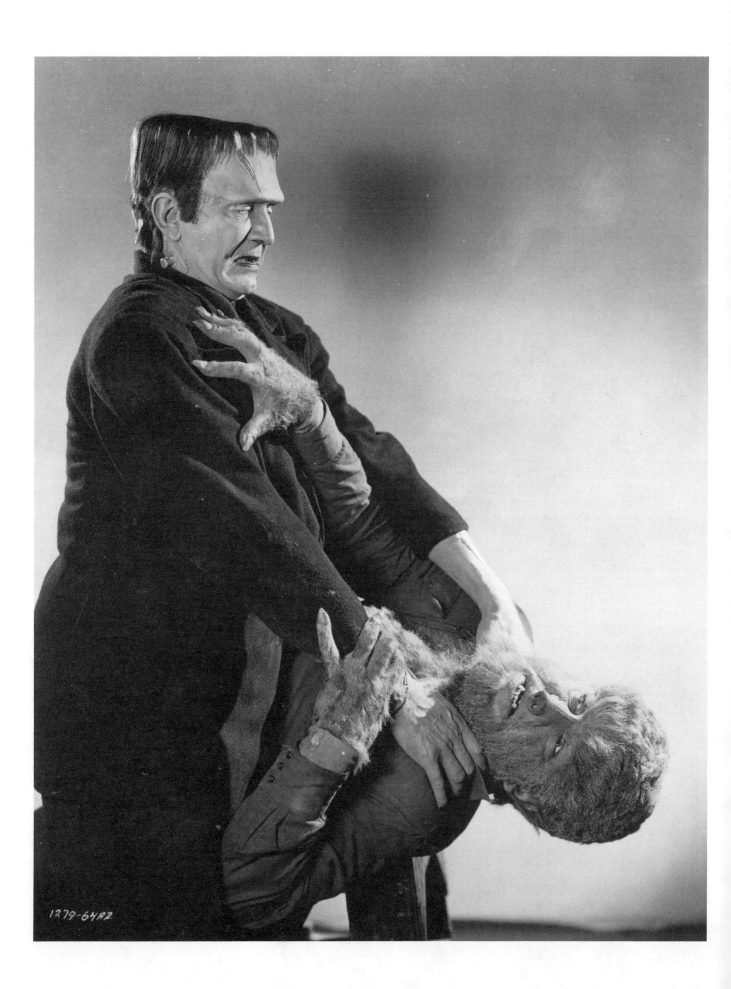

1279-64A2.

"W O L F M A N   M E E T S   F R A N K E N S T E I N"

SCREENPLAY

by

Curt Siodmak

```
  *
 ***
*****
 ***
  *
```

(Revised 3/31/42

Curt Siodmak
Three Rivers
California

(Revised 3/31/42)   Curt Siodmak

7 + Contract file

"WOLF-MAN MEETS FRANKENSTEIN"

FADE IN:

1   EXT. - THE WELSH MOUNTAINS - LONG - <u>NIGHT</u> -
     (MINIATURE)

     The pale moon, a diffused halo around its yellow
     disk, peers through low-hanging clouds at a Welsh
     valley, embedded between dark, barren hills. A
     howling wind rages over the sloping peaks, whistles
     through leafless trees, whines through the low brush
     thickly covering the dark earth.
     Crouched in the round saddle of a hill, a graveyard
     hides its crumbling walls behind a thin veil of
     floating haze...

                                        DISSOLVE TO:

2   EXT. - MOUNTAINS - LONG - <u>NIGHT</u>

     Two lonely wanderers - one lean, one bulky - grope
     their way toward the wrought-iron gates of the for-
     lorn burial place. The bulky one carries tools,
     the other a lantern.

3   EXT. - MOUNTAINS - MED. CLOSE - <u>NIGHT</u>

     His face muffled by the high collar of his flutter-
     ing cloak, the lean man swings a dark lantern,
     opening its shutter from time to time to light the
     narrow pass which winds up to the graveyard. The
     yellow glare of the lantern shines like the beam
     of a distant lighthouse through the gray mist.
     The bulky man carries some tools.

4   EXT. - THE GRAVEYARD - MED. CLOSE - <u>NIGHT</u>

The two men enter furtively through the creaking
wrought-iron gate. The angry WIND FANS it behind
them, and the rusty HINGES WHINE like wandering
souls. For a moment the men stop in their tracks,
held by a terror which grips their throats and
paralyzes their movements. But then the lean one
pushes his companion forward, toward a small
mausoleum, a round weather-beaten edifice, which
stands between the gray tombs, half-sunken into
the earth.
THE CAMERA FOLLOWS THEM, THEN PANS UP to the top
of the mausoleum. Deeply chiseled into the rounded
granite over the entrance is the name:

                    T A L B O T

CAMERA PANS DOWN to the door - old oak barred with
iron bands, - as if the dead who sleep inside wanted
to safeguard their treasures from the greedy world.

The two men come close to the forbidding door,
their lamp shining on it for a moment. Then the
light moves to a small window above it. The lean
one points at the stained-glass panes. The bulky
one lifts the lean one up to the window, first dropping his tools.

5   EXT. MAUSOLEUM - CLOSE ON WINDOW - <u>NIGHT</u>

The lean man, held by his bulky comrade, smashes the
stained-glass with his lantern, bending and tearing
the leaden frames until the opening is big enough
for him to squeeze through. While the bulky one
holds the lantern, then, the other crawls through
the broken window, sliding his thin body deftly into
the gap.

6   INT. MAUSOLEUM - MED. CLOSE NEAR WINDOW AND DOOR -
     <u>NIGHT</u>

The lean man's body comes down, feet first. Then,
supporting himself on the oaken bar inside the door,
he first takes the lamp from his friend's hand, and
the tools, then helps him to squeeze his bulky body
through the hole. The latter moans in distress as
the sharp glass pricks through his clothes. He comes
down head-first, his friend catching him just in time
to prevent him from crashing on to the stone floor.

7 INT. MAUSOLEUM - ANOTHER ANGLE - NIGHT

The lean man opens the shutter on his lantern and directs its yellow beam over the gray stone sarcophagi.

CAMERA PANS: Tombs made of stone fill the round vault with their timeless presence. One each tomb is an engraved plate, bearing the name of some member of the Talbot family, back to the Middle Ages. The light of the lantern wanders along the faded inscriptions; here and there, names are revealed as the light passes:

JOHN TALBOT - 1352 to 1402

LAWRENCE AND ANNE TALBOT - 1465 to 1521

OVER COMES THE VOICE of the lean one, whispering. A strange ECHO reverberates back from ceiling and walls, as if a dozen frightened men were speaking:

                    VOICE OF THE LEAN ONE
          "John Talbot"... "Lawrence and
          Anne Talbot"... "Martin Talbot
          1837... "Elizabeth Talbot 1845"...

CAMERA CONTINUES TO PAN, as the lantern light in the hand of the lean one wanders to a tomb of recent origin. Light and CAMERA STOP AND FOCUS on it:

                    VOICE OF THE LEAN ONE (cont'd)
          "Lawrence Stewart Talbot,
          who died at the youthful age
          of thirty-one. R. I. P."...

The light from the lantern becomes brighter as the two men approach the tomb. Both enter the PICTURE.

                    THE LEAN ONE
          That's it!

He puts the lamp on top of the stone tomb and says:

                    THE LEAN ONE (cont'd)
          Give me the chisel -

The CLANG of steel on stone is heard as the bulky one puts the tools on the sarcophagus and he asks in a frightened voice:

                                        CONTINUED

7   CONTINUED:

                              THE BULKY ONE
                    Suppose they didn't bury him
                    with the money on him?

The lean one begins to work on the granite slab
in the front of the tomb. The NOISE of his HAMMER-
ING awakens a thousand ECHOES. He pauses, gestures
impatiently:

                              THE LEAN ONE
                    Everybody in the village knows
                    about it - his gold watch and
                    diamond ring - and money in his
                    pockets...

He bends down and picks up a steel lever. The bulky
one, to give himself courage and the conviction that
they're not doing wrong, says:

                              THE BULKY ONE
                    It's a sin to bury good money
                    in bad earth - when it could
                    help people...

                              THE LEAN ONE
                         (as he works)
                    Rich folk have no feeling
                    for the poor!

He puts the lever into the hole he has chiseled out
of the stone and tries to lift the lid off the tomb:

                              THE LEAN ONE (cont'd)
                    Come on...

The bulky one puts all his weight behind the lever
and slowly the lid begins to move. The men pause
a moment, to gather new strength.

8   INT. MAUSOLEUM - CLOSE NEAR TOMB - ANOTHER ANGLE -
     NIGHT

The bulky one says with a shudder:

                                        CONTINUED

8   CONTINUED:

> BULKY ONE
> This gives me the creeps. -
> What do you think it'll look
> like - after so many years?

> LEAN ONE
> Just bones - and an empty skull!

With all his strength, he pushes the granite slab
which glides off the tomb and hits the ground with
a terrific CRASH. For seconds the sound ECHOES
between the walls. The men stand motionless,
petrified, until quiet falls again on the semi-
dark vault. Then they start to look into the tomb.

9   INT. MAUSOLEUM - CLOSE ON TOMB - NIGHT

It is open now and we see that there is a top layer
of dried leaves and shriveled flowers, covering
the body of a man.

The lean one boldly approaches the tomb and picks up
a handful of the dried flowers and leaves which fill
the coffin. The bulky one holds up the lamp with
trembling hands, to light the scene:

> LEAN ONE
> (puzzled)
> Wolf-bane!

As he removes the leaves, we see the rotting shoes
of the "corpse". Then, as he pulls out more and
more of the crumbling foliage with both hands, the
form of a man, fully clothed, becomes visible.

Faster and faster the lean one pushes away the dried
leaves, driven by greed and avarice. Then the lamp
in the bulky man's hand begins to sway:

> BULKY ONE
> (terrified)
> Look!

The lean one stops and stares:

10   CLOSE ON THE HANDS IN THE TOMB

Folded over a human chest, are hands without a sign
of decay, smooth hands of a living human being.
The nails have grown very long. On the second
finger of the left hand, a broad golden ring,
diamond-set, mirrors the light of the lantern like
a small captive sun.

CAMERA PULLS BACK to include the two men looking
into the tomb. The lean one notices only the ring
and says greedily:

LEAN ONE
See - the ring - I told you!

He stretches out his hand to grab the ring - but
the bulky one holds him back by the shoulder:

BULKY ONE
You said he'd be nothing
but bones!

The lean one stops, aghast at this revelation, but
then he says:

LEAN ONE
(nervously)
The air in here - it's kept
him like that -

Overcoming his fear, he brushes off the rest of the
leaves.

The man's face appears - a quiet face, deadly pale.
He has a bandage around his forehead, as if having
died of a head wound. But his expression seems to
be that of a man sleeping.

BULKY ONE
(fearfully)
He looks like he's asleep...

11   INT. MAUSOLEUM - CLOSE ON TOMB - REVERSE ANGLE -
NIGHT

The bulky one moves closer with his lamp, his fear
gradually replaced by greed, lest he might not get
his full share of the loot. The light shines
brightly on the "corpse".

CONTINUED

11   CONTINUED:

                    BULKY ONE
          Now for the pockets...

He stretches out his free hand, but the lean one
pushes him away:

                    LEAN ONE
              First the ring -

He grabs Lawrence Talbot's hand, to pull off the
precious piece of gold.

                    LEAN ONE (cont'd)
              We won't have to worry
              for a long time -

The dead man's arm, hand and fingers move supplely
under the pull of the lean one. The bulky one becomes frightened again:

                    BULKY ONE
          I thought the dead were stiff!

                    LEAN ONE
          Shut up!

He straightens the fingers of the hand in front of
him, takes off the ring and grunts with delight:

                    LEAN ONE (cont'd)
          Gold!

Suddenly he stands petrified, his face frozen with
fear.

12   CLOSE DOWN SHOT ON HANDS IN COFFIN

      The dead man's hand closes - its fingers snap around
      the lean one's wrist!

13   CLOSE AT TOMB

      The lean one, deathly pale, utters one cry of terror
      and agony - then almost swoons. The bulky one, his
      eyes protruding from their sockets, stares at his
      friend - as he sees the hand of the corpse closed
      around his companion's wrist!

                                        CONTINUED

13   CONTINUED:

                                    LEAN ONE
                    It's holding me! -

He drops the ring -

14   CLOSE DOWN SHOT

as the ring falls on the floor and rolls away.

15   MED. CLOSE AT TOMB - <u>NIGHT</u>

With his free hand, the lean one tries to break the
deadly grip around his wrist. He whines and wriggles
his thin body in futile attempts to free himself from
the corpse.

                                    LEAN ONE
                                  (in agony)
                    Help me!

But the bulky one is too terrified to do anything but
stare and stammer:

                                    BULKY ONE
                    Alive!...

Suddenly the lamp drops out of his trembling hand.
It crashes to the floor.

16   CLOSE DOWN SHOT

As the lantern drops, the glass breaks, and the ig-
nited oil runs out, like a fiery snake running quickly
across the granite floor.

17   INT. MAUSOLEUM - MED. FULL - <u>NIGHT</u>

The lean one struggles and cries out. The bulky one,
in nameless terror, dashes toward the door, jumping
over the flame, while the lean one whimpers, half-
insane with fear and pain:

                                    LEAN ONE
                    Help.... Help...!

                                        CONTINUED

17   CONTINUED:

But the bulky one climbs up quickly to the window.
His terror makes his body supple and he squeezes
through the broken window, without any concern for
his companion's fate. He disappears head-first,
while the lean one, in a terrible voice, continues
to cry out.

18   CLOSE AT TOMB - <u>NIGHT</u>

The lean one still struggling to free himself, but
the dead man's fist holds him in a grip of steel.

                    LEAN ONE
                (more weakly and
                   despairingly)
            Don't leave me...!

19   MAUSOLEUM - MED. FULL - <u>NIGHT</u>

The burning oil throws flickering silhouettes over
the moist walls. The shadow of the lean one sways
to and fro...

20   EXT. MAUSOLEUM - MED. CLOSE - <u>NIGHT</u>

The bulky one climbs through the window. Torn
pieces from his cloak flutter like mourning flags
from the broken window-frame. His face is bleeding,
his hands are cut by the glass. Recklessly he jumps
to the ground. Then, picking himself up, he limps
away as fast as his weak legs can carry him.

CAMERA PANS UP TO THE WINDOW: The flames of the
burning oil blaze away inside the mausoleum, then
start to die down slowly.

As THE CAMERA HOLDS ON THIS a moment, we HEAR THE
VOICE OF THE LEAN ONE. His whimpering CRIES are
gradually drowned out by the HOWLING OF THE STORM...

                                   SLOW FADE OUT:

FADE IN:

21   EXT. - THE TOWN OF CARDIFF - LONG - <u>NIGHT</u>

A mist, saturated with coal dust, hangs over the
town of Cardiff. A few lights shine through the
night, as through a dark veil. The deep FOG HORNS
of cargo boats wail mournfully from the distant
harbor.

DISSOLVE TO:

22   EXT. - STREET NEAR THE HARBOR - MED. LONG - <u>NIGHT</u>

The SIRENS of the ships SOUND CLOSER, the SPLUTTER
of their slow-moving PROPELLERS comes from the nearby wharf. A few CRANES are SHRIEKING in high-
pitched voices. The RUMBLE of their chains pene-
trates the quiet night.

A police "Bobby" patrols the empty street. His
steps ring with a hollow SOUND between the low,
coal-blackened houses. Suddenly he stops - sees:

23   EXT. - HARBOR STREET - MED. LONG - <u>NIGHT</u>

The constable sees a man lying on the pavement,
his feet sprawled out, his head hidden in his arms.
Any passing car might run over him in the semi-
darkness.
CAMERA DOLLIES with the Bobby, as he approaches
the prostrate figure hurriedly.
CAMERA STOPS in MED. CLOSE: The constable looks
at the body of the man in front of him, whom he can
hear breathing heavily. Taking his truncheon from
its holster, the Bobby says harshly:

           CONSTABLE
     Here, now! Come off it!

But the man does not answer. Only his labored
breathing IS HEARD. The Bobby bends down to the
quiet figure and touches him with his truncheon:

CONTINUED

23   CONTINUED:

CONSTABLE (cont'd)
Get on with you! You've got
a home, haven't you?... Or
would you rather come along
to the station?

As the man does not answer, the constable turns
him over rudely.

24   CLOSE TWO SHOT - GROUND - NIGHT

The constable looks into the man's face. It is
gray, unconscious. The man's head is still bandaged, but through the raggedy soiled linen, a big
spot of blood has penetrated. The face - the eyes
are half-closed - now shows an expression of agony
and the teeth are bared in pain. It is Larry.

CONSTABLE
Blimey!

CAMERA PULLS BACK AND UP as the policeman straightens up quickly and looks around for help. He takes
out his whistle and blows it - once - twice - three
times... As he bends back toward the body -

DISSOLVE TO:

25   EXT. - HOSPITAL IN CARDIFF - LONG - NIGHT

The windows of the building are partly lit up.
An ambulance drives through the gates.

26   MED. CLOSE AT HOSPITAL ENTRANCE - NIGHT

The ambulance drives up to the reception door and
stops. The assistants jump down, open the ambulance
door and take out a stretcher bearing the unconscious
body of Larry.

DISSOLVE TO:

27   INT. OPERATING THEATRE - CLOSE SHOT OF LARRY'S FACE
      - DAY

He is unconscious still; his head is bandaged anew.
CAMERA PULLS BACK: Lying on a stretcher, he is
wheeled out of the operating theatre by an assistant, while a surgeon (DOCTOR HARLEY) takes off his
mouth-piece, rips off his gloves, and wipes the beads
of sweat from his forehead.
The surgeon walks toward the CAMERA. He is a man of
about thirty-eight, youthful-looking, but fatigued
now. His assistant, a man younger than he, walks at
his side. As they approach the CAMERA, CAMERA DOLLIES
BACK, keeping the same distance:

                    ASSISTANT
          What do you make of it,
          Doctor Harley?

                    DR. HARLEY
                    (shrugs)
          The man should have died
          hours ago... A sharp instrument
          must have penetrated the inner
          table - there's a compound
          fracture of...

His VOICE BECOMES FAINTER and FADES OUT, as we

                                        DISSOLVE TO:

28   INT. OFFICE IN THE CARDIFF HOSPITAL - MED. CLOSE - DAY

Two plain-clothes policemen are examining Larry's
clothes. One of the men is Inspector OWEN, of the
local constabulary, the other is a sergeant. They
are assisted by a nurse.
The shoes, shirt, coat and trousers are spread out
on a table. While the assistant takes notes, Owen
dictates his official report:

                    OWEN
          A coat - with no identifying
          marks. Trousers - of the same
          pattern. Material - expensive,
          cut by a first-class tailor...

The door opens and Doctor Harley enters. The men
turn toward him. Owen drops Larry's coat, which he
had picked up:

                                        CONTINUED

28   CONTINUED:

                    OWEN (cont'd)
          Good morning, Doctor Harley -

Harley approaches them, tired, still in his white
smock:

                    HARLEY
          'Morning, Inspector -

                    OWEN
          Any news for me?

                    HARLEY
          Operation - successful...
                    (with a smile)
          the patient's still alive!

                    OWEN
                    (half-kidding)
          Harley, the miracle-man, eh?

Harley sighs wearily and takes off his smock:

                    HARLEY
          I hope you're right...
                    (nods toward
                     clothes)
          Found out anything about
          him yet, Inspector?

Owen shrugs his shoulders and turns toward the clothes
again.

29   HOSPITAL OFFICE - REVERSE ANGLE

as the men look at Larry's clothes:

                    OWEN
          Rotten - as if they'd been
          buried for years! Have a
          look at these mouldy spots -
                    (pointing)
          and the shoes - the leather
          is slimy...
                    (he looks closer
                     and reads)
          "Made in U. S. A."...

                              CONTINUED

29   CONTINUED:

                              HARLEY
              There's a clue!

Owen shakes his head:

                         OWEN
              American shoes are sold every-
              where... They're no proof he's
              a Yank...

He picks up the shirt, which falls apart at his
touch, as if it were woven of spider's thread:

                         OWEN (cont'd)
              Obviously, these things were
              picked up from some refuse
              pile...
                    (then, with a sigh)
                         HARLEY
              I'd like to have a look at
              him... You don't mind, Doctor?

                         HARLEY
              Not at all. Come along with me...

He walks to the door, followed by Owen.

                         HARLEY (cont'd)
              But you'll find him still
              unconscious...

30   INT. CORRIDOR OF THE HOSPITAL - MED. CLOSE ON DOOR

      of Larry's room. The door opens and a nurse steps
      out hastily, an expression of utter astonishment on
      her pale face. Looking back into the room at the
      patient (o.s.), she is just closing the door when
      Dr. Harley and Inspector Owen step into the PICTURE.
      The nurse turns:

                         HARLEY
              How's the patient?

                         NURSE
              He's conscious, Doctor Harley.
              He talked!

                                        CONTINUED

30   CONTINUED:

                         HARLEY
                      (dumbfounded)
                Conscious? And talked!
                But that's impossible so soon
                after such a critical operation!

He opens the door and enters the room, followed by
Owen.

31   INT. HOSPITAL ROOM - MED. CLOSE - DAY

        Larry sits motionless in his bed, propped up on the
        pillows, his forehead still bandaged. His hands are
        limp on the sheet. His eyes stare toward CAMERA and
        turn slowly toward the door as Harley and Owen enter.

32   MED. CLOSE - ANOTHER ANGLE

        Harley, followed by Owen, step toward Larry. The
        doctor looks at his patient with astonishment:

                         HARLEY
                Hullo! Nurse tells me you're
                well enough to talk -

                         LARRY
                      (speaking with
                       difficulty)
                Yes, doctor...

        Harley steps close to the bed and takes the patient's
        pulse:

                         HARLEY
                Pulse seventy-two...
                No fever...

        He turns to Owen and shakes his head, mystified,
        then turns back to Larry, asking:

                         HARLEY (cont'd)
                No pain?

                         LARRY
                No...

        He looks at Harley with eyes devoid of any expression
        and asks:

                                        CONTINUED

32   CONTINUED:

                              LARRY (cont'd)
            How did I get here?

                              HARLEY
            You were found in the street,
            more dead than alive, with a
            head injury...

Larry looks toward the window, then back to the
doctor and asks wonderingly:

                              LARRY
            Where am I?

                              HARLEY
            At Cardiff Hospital...
            Didn't the nurse tell you?

                              LARRY
                      (wonderingly)
            Cardiff...

Harley watches him carefully. As Larry's eyes
wander to Owen, the Inspector cuts in:

                              OWEN
            How did you get that skull
            fracture?

Larry looks at him blankly:

                              LARRY
            I don't remember...

Harley asks another question, very kindly and
patiently, so as not to upset Larry:

                              HARLEY
            This is Inspector Owen and
            I am Doctor Harley. What's
            your name?

Larry's face contorts; he puts his hands slowly to
his head:

                              LARRY
            Lawrence Talbot...

                                        CONTINUED

32   CONTINUED - (2):

Owen's face lights up and he repeats the name so
as not to forget it:

OWEN
Lawrence Talbot! And where
do you come from?

LARRY
Llanwelly Village... How
did I get to Cardiff?

He suddenly seems to remember dreadful happenings
and becomes agitated. Harley puts his hand on
Larry's arm soothingly:

HARLEY
That's enough for today -
you'd better rest. -
You'll be fit very soon,
Talbot... Come along, Inspector -

The men start to leave, Owen somewhat reluctantly,
but Harley takes his arm. -
Larry looks after them, unheeding, as if his mind
were far away already, lost in dim but terrible
recollections...

DISSOLVE TO:

33   OFFICE IN CARDIFF HOSPITAL - MED. CLOSE - DAY

(Same set as in Scene 29) Doctor Harley sits behind his desk, thoughtfully smoking his pipe. He
is dressed in a business suit. Sitting in front of
the desk, with his hat on, is Inspector Owen. He
has pulled the telephone over to him and is speaking
into it:

OWEN
(into phone)
Put me through to the police
station at Llanwelly Village...

Holding his hand over the mouth-piece, he says to
Harley:

CONTINUED

33   CONTINUED:

                    OWEN
                 (casually)
          The usual routine check-up,
          Doctor - and then we can
          close the case.

The doctor is not so sure it will be that easy...
He gets up and strides back and forth, as Owen
speaks into the phone:

                    OWEN (cont'd)
                 (phoning)
          Llanwelly police station?
          This is Inspector Owen speaking,
          from Cardiff... Have you anything
          in your files on a man named -

                                        CUT TO:

34   INT. POLICE STATION - CLOSE ON DESK - DAY

Behind the desk in this drab little station, a
typical country police sergeant is on the wire.
Beside him stands a policeman.

                    SERGEANT
                 (into phone)
          Lawrence Talbot? Of course -
          he lived here -

                                        CUT TO:

35   CARDIFF OFFICE - BACK TO OWEN AT PHONE - HARLEY NEARBY

                    OWEN
                 (phoning)
          Well then, it's all right -
          we have him here in our
          hospital -

                                        CUT BACK TO:

36   SERGEANT AND POLICEMAN

The sergeant frowns and shakes his head wonderingly:

                    SERGEANT
                    (amused)
          I shouldn't want him in
          our hospital... He died
          four years ago!

He listens for a moment and continues:

                    SERGEANT (cont'd)
          Of course I'm sure, Inspector!
          I was present at the funeral -

                                        BACK TO:

37   HOSPITAL OFFICE - OWEN AND HARLEY

Owen puts down the receiver and says to Harley, sadly:

                    OWEN
          Lawrence Talbot died four
          years ago. Your man is an
          imposter.

                    HARLEY
          That's a harsh word - for
          a poor devil of unsound mind.

                    OWEN
                    (sarcastic)
          I'll wager he's sound enough
          to remember his own name!
          Just let me have another talk
          with him -

He walks toward the door but Harley holds him back.

                    HARLEY
          That man is my patient - not
          your prisoner. I'll decide
          when he can be questioned again!

Owen looks at the doctor, shrugs his shoulders and
pulls at his hat:

                    OWEN
          Very well - it's in your hands...

                                        DISSOLVE TO:

38   EXT. - SKY - <u>NIGHT</u> - FROM HOSPITAL WINDOW - LONG

The full moon, partly hidden by fast-moving clouds.
A WIND IS HOWLING.
From afar, the deep mournful SOUND of a SHIP'S
SIREN comes through the night.

CAMERA PANS DOWN and PULLS BACK into Larry's room
in the Cardiff hospital. We HOLD on Larry lying
in his bed, asleep. The upper part of his body is
propped up on pillows. The room is half-dark...

Now - like the hand of a clock, a beam of moonlight
falls into the room. Then, as the unseen clouds
race past the moon, the beam of light seems to
broaden, wander along the floor, climb up the bed
and touch Larry's face with deep shadows.

39   INT. LARRY'S ROOM - CLOSE - <u>NIGHT</u> - (TRICK SHOT)

Slowly Larry's face changes: a fulvous growth
appears on the cheeks, on the forehead, on the hands
which lie motionless on the sheet. The mouth en-
larges and long wolf-teeth hang like fangs over the
parted lips.

And in his sleep, the wolf-man utters a low grunt.
Then it stirs, opens luminous eyes.

The beam of the moonlight fades away, as if having
accomplished its task.

Then, in the half-dark, the phantom moves, throws
back the cover of its bed...

                                        DISSOLVE TO:

40   EXT. CORNER OF A STREET IN CARDIFF - MED. FULL -
<u>NIGHT</u>

The street is deserted, as the constable makes his
rounds. (Same "Bobby" as seen in 22)

The full moon throws lambent shadows over the
cobblestones.

The lonely patrolman's steps ECHO back from the dark
house walls. Suddenly he stops - sees:

41   STREET - MED. CLOSE - NIGHT

The strange silhouette of a giant form - half-man,
half-wolf - is thrown over the pavement by the pale
light of the moon.

The constable comes into scene. Not trusting his
eyes, he cries out:

                    CONSTABLE
          Who's there?

He grabs his truncheon - but before he can unloosen
the weapon, the Thing behind the corner leaps forward and grabs him with its long claws.

42   EXT. - STREET - MED. CLOSE - ANOTHER ANGLE

Attacked off guard, the constable succumbs. The
wolf-man pulls its helpless victim behind the corner
- out of our sight. The constable's muffled CRIES
of agony ARE HEARD.

43   EXT. - STREET - CAMERA ON GROUND - FOCUSSING ON CORNER

The shadows of the wolf-man dance over the cobblestones, the limp body of its victim in its hairy
arms. Then the constable's helmet rolls toward the
CAMERA, enlarging until it fills the screen, black-
ing out our view...

                                        FADE OUT:

FADE IN:

44   INT. LARRY'S HOSPITAL ROOM - CLOSE ON WINDOW SILL -
      MORNING

The window is open. On the sill lies Larry's head-
bandage. The nurse's VOICE COMES OVER:

                    NURSE'S VOICE
                    (in a whisper)
          It was here this morning when
          I came in. I didn't open the
          window - he must have done it
          himself -

                                        CONTINUED

44   CONTINUED:

CAMERA PANS to the bed where Larry lies on his back,
fast asleep, in his pajamas and bare feet. But the
bed covers are on the floor, as if thrown off in
great haste...

45   HOSPITAL ROOM - MED. CLOSE - HARLEY, NURSE AND LARRY

                    HARLEY
            We'd better cover him up...

They approach Larry from opposite sides of the bed,
pulling his body gently into position, picking up
the covers and smoothing them over him.

Larry is breathing heavily, his eyes closed. Suddenly he wakes up, in terror, and looks at Harley:

                    HARLEY
                (in a friendly
                  tone)
            You're all right -
            nothing has happened...

Larry stares at him as if he hadn't understood.
Harley turns to the nurse:

                    HARLEY
            Get me some bandages -
            we'll renew the compress...

As the nurse leaves, Larry sits up, a terrified look
on his face. Harley takes his arm to feel his pulse:

                    HARLEY
            Don't get excited, please.
            Be calm...

                    LARRY
                (stammers)
            Doctor - Harley! Something
            terrible happened to me in
            the night! -

                    HARLEY
            A nightmare, most likely, -
            you must have been walking
            in your sleep...

But Larry stares at him in mounting terror.

46   INT. HOSPITAL ROOM - CLOSE ON LARRY AND HARLEY

                    LARRY
              Call the police!

                    HARLEY
                   (surprised)
              The police?

Larry tries to get up but Harley pushes him back
gently:

                    LARRY
              Call the police -
              I'm a murderer!

To calm him down, Harley says quietly, as he rings
a bell near the bed:

                    HARLEY
              Of course - anything you say...

We HEAR the DOOR OPEN and the nurse enters.
Harley turns to her and orders:

                    HARLEY (cont'd)
              Ask Inspector Owen to
              come here at once.

The nurse leaves - we HEAR the DOOR CLOSE again.
Larry is looking at Harley with a gleam of insanity
in his eyes. But Harley smiles at him reassuringly:

                    HARLEY
              Now what's all this about
              wanting the police?

                    LARRY
                   (slowly)
              I killed a man...

Harley continues to use a friendly tone, to keep
the patient calm:

                    HARLEY
              Do you want to tell me
              about it?

                    LARRY
              Last night... I killed
              a constable...

.CONTINUED

46   CONTINUED:

Harley looks at him quizzically, not believing him:

                    HARLEY
          But you were in this room
          all night.

                    LARRY
               (persistently)
          I killed that man...

                    HARLEY
               (smiling)
          You couldn't have - you
          must have heard the nurses
          talking about it -

                    LARRY
               (doggedly)
          I did it...

                    HARLEY
          Mr. Talbot, you're suffering
          from a delusion. The fact is,
          it happened blocks from here.
          Moreover, he was killed by
          some sort of wild animal -

                    LARRY
               (wildly)
          It was I! I change into an
          animal - at night - when the
          moon is full... I crawl on
          all fours - and kill!

Harley watches him intently, gravely. The DOOR IS
HEARD TO OPEN AGAIN and they look toward it as Owen
walks into the shot.

47   HOSPITAL ROOM - ANOTHER ANGLE - THE THREE

                    OWEN
               (sarcastic)
          Well, Mr. Talbot, did you
          decide to remember who you are?

Harley sees that Larry doesn't like Owen. Afraid
that Owen might further upset his patient, the
doctor says:

                                        CONTINUED

47   CONTINUED:

                    HARLEY
          Mr. Talbot seems to have heard
          about the unfortunate constable
          last night... It's disturbed him -

Larry stares at the Inspector, determined to make
him believe what he thinks is the truth:

                    LARRY
               (with anguish)
          No - you don't understand!
          It's the curse on me ---
          I change into a wolf!

Owen, disappointed by this fantastic "confession"
of a disordered mind, looks at Harley, puzzled.
Then he decides to humor Larry:

                    OWEN
          That's a bit difficult to
          believe, my good man -

Larry, furious at his unbelief, sits up in his bed,
tears open his shirt, and points to the scar on his
chest:

                    LARRY
               (desperately trying
                to convince them)
          See this scar? - It's where a
          wolf bit me once - only he wasn't
          a real wolf - he was a man, a
          gypsy. A werewolf! I killed him -
          and his curse passed on to me.
          Now I change into a wolf - at
          night - when the moon is full...

Owen looks at Harley again, significantly, as if
doubting Larry's insanity. Larry catches the glance:

                    LARRY (cont'd)
          It's the truth! Ask Maleva -
          she'll tell you -

Owen pounces on the name:

                    OWEN
          Maleva? Who is she?

                              CONTINUED

                    LARRY
          A gypsy woman - she knows
          all about the curse. Ask her -

                    OWEN
               (disappointed again)
          A gypsy woman... Maleva...

Harley motions to Owen not to say any more, then
turns to Larry:

                    HARLEY
          You'd better rest now, Talbot -

But Larry suddenly throws off the bed-clothes and
puts his feet on the floor:

                    LARRY
               (shouting in
                desperation)
          Are you blind - all of you?
          Why won't you believe me?

                    HARLEY
               (soothingly)
          Yes, of course... But please
          lie down and calm yourself.
          Let's discuss your case quietly -

But Larry refuses to be swerved. He jumps up off
the bed, towering over the two men:

                    LARRY
          Why do you let me go on
          murdering? Why don't you
          help me?

                    OWEN
               (coldly)
          Just tell us your real name -
          and let us worry about the rest!

                    LARRY
               (pleading)
          I told you! Talbot -
          Lawrence Talbot -

                                        CONTINUED

47   CONTINUED - (2): 3

                          OWEN
                       (cruelly)
                  Lawrence Talbot died four
                  years ago!

48   LARRY'S ROOM - ANOTHER ANGLE - FAVORING LARRY

Harley is distressed - he didn't want Owen to mention
Larry's "death" - but it's too late now to stop him.
Larry stares at Owen, unnerved, his jaw trembling:

                          LARRY
                  Four years?

He looks at his hands and shakes his head in terror:

                          LARRY (cont'd)
                  I didn't die...

Then he stares at the two men and cries out in a
hoarse voice:

                          LARRY (cont'd)
                  I can't die - as long as the
                  curse is on me! It drives me
                  to roam the earth - like a
                  wild beast - and kill...
                       (breaking down)
                  Don't let me kill again!
                  Take care of me!

Owen and Harley are visibly affected by Larry's
strange outburst. Owen tries to hide his fear, as
Larry comes toward him, a powerful figure, wild-eyed:

                          LARRY (cont'd)
                  You must believe me -
                  save me...!

Harley rings a bell four times, then steps between
Larry and Owen:

                          HARLEY
                       (firmly)
                  If you want us to help you,
                  Talbot, you must do as we say.
                  Now lie down...

Continued

48 CONTINUED:

Harley takes Larry's arm - but Larry jerks himself
free:

>   LARRY
>   You think I'm insane, don't you?
>   You think I don't know what I'm
>   talking about... Well - just look
>   in the grave where they think
>   they buried Lawrence Talbot!
>   Find out if there's a body in it -

49 LARRY'S ROOM - MED. CLOSE

The door opens and three husky male nurses enter,
in response to the doctor's ring:

>   HARLEY
>   Please get back into your
>   bed, Mr. Talbot.

Larry steps back, snarling, and the doctor nods
to the men who advance on him the patient:

>   LARRY
>   (defiantly)
>   You think you can treat me
>   like a lunatic! You're as
>   stupid as all the others!

He starts toward the window, which he pulls open,
ready to jump out. But the men pounce on him and
hold him back. Larry turns and starts to fight the
three men at once. Harley takes Owen by the arm and
leads him out, confident that his patient will be
subdued.

50 INT. CORRIDOR OF HOSPITAL - MED. CLOSE - HARLEY
AND OWEN - DAY

Harley closes the door of Larry's room and walks
away with Owen. The NOISE of the struggle between
Larry and the guards is HEARD through the door.
CAMERA TRUCKS in front of Harley and Owen as they
walk down corridor, talking:

CONTINUED

OWEN
(puzzled)
He told that pipe dream
quite convincingly. He
really believes it!

HARLEY
I'm afraid so. People with
brain injuries sometimes have
supernormal mental powers that
are quite extraordinary - as if
they could experience happenings
taking place miles away... We
call it "extra-sensory perception" -

OWEN
Then you mean to say Talbot
actually experienced the murder
last night?

HARLEY
(with a shrug)
Clairvoyantly - perhaps...
It's hard to say... Certainly
he got up and opened his window...
The border-line between delusion
and reality is very narrow. Unknowingly, a patient may over-
step that line...

OWEN
Then that man is dangerous!
He belongs behind bars.

HARLEY
He's a lycanthrope...

OWEN
A what?

HARLEY
A lycanthrope.

OWEN
What's that?

HARLEY
A man who imagines himself
to be a wolf...

CONTINUED

50   CONTINUED - (2):

Owen pauses in f.g. and looks wonderingly at Harley:

                    OWEN
                 (with pity)
          Poor devil... Wish I could do
          something to help him... I
          think I'll run up to Llenwelly
          and find out -

                    HARLEY
          I had the very same idea, In-
          spector. To be able to cure
          him, I have to know who he is...

                                    SLOW DISSOLVE TO

51   EXT. THE WELSH MOUNTAINS - LONG - LATE AFTERNOON

The sinking sun makes long shadows fall on the hill-
side, as four men make their way through the low brush
toward the graveyard. The wanderers are Dr. Harley,
Inspector Owen, the police sergeant from Llenwelly,
and the grave-digger.

52   MOUNTAINS - MED. CLOSE

Harley, in a short fur coat, shivers and jams his
hands into his square pockets. Owen wears a bowler
hat, spats, and the mackintosh of the English police.
The local sergeant is in uniform. Behind these men
trots the grave-digger, a stooped old fellow. Big
keys on an enormous ring hang from his work-hardened
hands.

The harsh wind, howling over the plain, makes the keys
CLANG. The men bend before the wind, nearly bowled
over.

They enter the church-yard through the CREEKING wrought-
iron gate - and walk toward the mausoleum.

53   EXT. MAUSOLEUM - MED. CLOSE

The group pauses, while the grave-digger approaches
the door with the big key. Owen points to the window
above the door. It is broken - and the remains of a
shredded coat wave from the smashed window-frame.

                                    CONTINUED

55   CONTINUED:

Owen shouts above the wind to the sergeant:

                    OWEN
          Somebody's broken into this
          vault... How long is it since
          you were here last, Sergeant?

                    SERGEANT
          Not for months... Nobody's
          died in Llanwelly lately -
          and nobody comes here if he
          doesn't have to...

The grave-digger meanwhile has been fumbling with
his keys. But before he can put the right key into
the key-hole, a heavy gust of wind presses against
the door, which CREAKS slowly on its hinges, and
reveals the interior of the dark, moist vault.

Owen is the first one to step toward the door. He
pushes it open wider with his rolled-up umbrella,
then taking a flash-light from his pocket, he enters.
The other men, Harley close behind him, follow.

54   INT. MAUSOLEUM - MED. CLOSE

The men enter and watch the beam of Owen's light
play over walls and sarcophagi. The beam of the
flash-light stops at Lawrence Talbot's tomb. And
there, at the foot of the tomb, lies the grotesquely
bent figure of a man ("the Lean One"). Owen's light
plays on the body.

                    OWEN
          Somebody - must have taken
          the - body - out of the tomb!

He approaches the stone tomb hesitantly, followed
by the local sergeant. The latter bends down over
the prone figure, then gets up quickly and announces:

                    SERGEANT
          That's not Lawrence Talbot!

Harley and the grave-digger, surprised, move closer
to the body.

55   MAUSOLEUM - CLOSE NEAR BODY OF LEAN ONE

Owen stands closest to the corpse (which we cannot
see now, as it is outside the PICTURE) - and says:

                    OWEN
                (astonished)
          Not Talbot?... I say!
          Do you know this man here?

                    SERGEANT
          Why, yes - it's Freddy Jolly!

                    OWEN
          Who's he?

                    SERGEANT
                (shrugging)
          A ne'er-do-well... been up
          for vagrancy and petty larceny -

Owen turns to Harley, asking:

                    OWEN
          What would you say the man
          died of, Doctor?

Harley bends down, examines the o.s. corpse, rises
and says:

                    HARLEY
          Severed jugular...
          He bled to death.

                    OWEN
                (hoarsely, hiding
                 his terror)
          Same as the constable in
          Cardiff!

                    HARLEY
          Yes... Seems to be the bite
          of an animal -

                    SERGEANT
                (nodding solemnly)
          Aye - that animal - we remember
          it well hereabouts! And it
          must have carried away the
          corpse of poor Sir Lawrence...

CONTINUED

55   CONTINUED:

Owen looks at the sergeant, in sudden alarm:

                    OWEN
          What animal?

                    SERGEANT
          Didn't you know, sir? There
          was a wild animal around here -
          a few years ago -- it killed
          people -- bit through their
          throats -- sucked their blood -

                    OWEN
          Did they kill it?

                    SERGEANT
          Sir John Talbot thought he did.
          He attacked it in the dark one
          night - or so he thought...
          But it was his son he killed -
          poor Lawrence...

                    OWEN
                 (after a pause)
          Where is John Talbot now?

                    SERGEANT
          Over there -
                 (points to
                  another tomb)
          - died of grief shortly after
          Sir Lawrence...

                    OWEN
                 (nervous)
          Let's get out of here...

He starts to turn toward door.

                    SERGEANT
          And this body, sir?

                    OWEN
                 (turning back,
                  sharply)
          Don't touch it - it's evidence...

                    SERGEANT
          Yes sir.

56   INT. MAUSOLEUM - WIDER ANGLE - THE FOUR MEN

Owen moves toward the door, when the grave-digger
speaks up in a feeble, squeaky voice, choked by
fear:

                    GRAVE-DIGGER
          The door! -

Owen looks at the door and plays his light on it:

                         OWEN
          What about it?

57   CLOSE ON DOOR OF MAUSOLEUM

The lock of the door has been ripped off the bolts
and is hanging down. The light of Owen's lamp becomes brighter as Owen enters the PICTURE:

                         OWEN
                    (in utter dismay)
          Broken from inside!

CAMERA PULLS BACK into MED. CLOSE, as Owen turns to
the others and Harley speaks:

                         HARLEY
          I - I'd like to see a photo-
          graph of Lawrence Talbot -

                         SERGEANT
          There's one in my office, sir...

                                   DISSOLVE TO:

58   INT. POLICE STATION IN LLENWELLY - MED. CLOSE

(Same set as in Scene 36) Harvey and Owen watch the
sergeant open a filing case and take out a photograph:

                         SERGEANT
          Here's Sir Lawrence -
                    (adding, in
                    low voice)
          - may his soul rest in peace...

                                   CONTINUED

58   CONTINUED:

Owen takes the picture. As he looks at it, his
face freezes. Then he hands the picture to Harley:

>   OWEN
>   (hoarsely)
> Look at that face, doctor!
> Isn't that our man in Cardiff?

Harley looks at the picture.

59   CLOSE ON THE PHOTOGRAPH HELD IN HARLEY'S HAND

It shows a younger, smiling Larry - somehow differ-
ent from the injured man as we have seen him.

CAMERA PULLS BACK to take in group.

>   HARLEY
> There's a fantastic similarity
> - though I wouldn't swear it's
> the same man...

>   OWEN
> It can't be the same man!
> If it were - I'd be off my top!

Harley puts the picture face-down on the desk.

>   HARLEY
> I think the Sergeant had better
> go back with us to Cardiff
> and see if he can positively
> identify -

>   OWEN
> That's the thing to do!

60   POLICE STATION - NEAR SERGEANT'S DESK

Harley walks over to the phone and asks the sergeant:

>   HARLEY
> Do you mind - I must call
> the hospital - check up on
> my patient's condition...

CONTINUED

60   CONTINUED:

                                    SERGEANT
                          Of course, Doctor - go
                          right ahead.

Harley starts to use the phone:

                                    HARLEY
                          Hullo - please connect me
                          with the hospital in Cardiff -

As he waits, Owen turns to the sergeant and asks:

                                    OWEN
                          Did you ever hear of a
                          gypsy woman named Maleva?

The sergeant is at a loss at first, then he begins
to remember. He walks over to the files again and
takes out a registry-book:

                                    SERGEANT
                          A gypsy woman? Vagrant, eh?
                          We always register 'em...

He turns the pages, looking through the index:

                                    OWEN
                               (repeating)
                          Maleva was her name...

                                    SERGEANT
                          Yes... here she is...
                          Passed through town a few
                          years ago...

Then he suddenly stares at Owen - his mouth dropping
open, as if an idea had hit him. At the same moment,
Harley is heard at phone:

                                    HARLEY
                               (phoning)
                          Cardiff Hospital? Please
                          connect me with Doctor Gordon...

The sergeant continues with what he was saying to Owen:

                                                        CONTINUED

60   CONTINUED - (2):

                         SERGEANT
            She was in town the very same
            time that beast was prowling
            about! I remember now -
            she saw Sir Lawrence die...

As he and Owen look at each other wonderingly,
baffled by the strange case, we hear Dr. Harley
speaking again on phone:

                         HARLEY
            Doctor Gordon? This is Harley
            speaking... How's Lawrence
            Talbot doing? You know, the
            head injury case - who went
            violent yesterday -
                         (he listens,
                         very grave)

At the same time, Owen is looking at the registry-
book and saying to the sergeant:

                         OWEN
            We've got to trace her -
            find out what she knows
            about the whole business...

                         SERGEANT
            They're usually up here in
            Autumn. Summers they move
            back to the continent - the
            whole tribe...

Harley speaks into phone again:

                         HARLEY
                         (phoning)
            I'll be back tonight, Gordon...
            You've informed the police,
            I take it -
                         (listens again)
            Of course - that's all we can
            do at present. Goodbye.

He puts down the receiver and turns toward the others:

61   POLICE STATION - ANOTHER ANGLE - THE THREE MEN

Owen looks at Harley as if expecting bad news:

                              OWEN
                    What happened -
                    did he die?

                              HARLEY
                         (with a harsh
                          dry laugh)
                    No - Talbot tore off his
                    straight-jacket during the
                    night and escaped!

                              OWEN
                    Tore off the straight-
                    jacket! But how?

He stares at Harley, open-mouthed - and so does
the sergeant:

                              HARLEY
                    He bit right through it -
                    tore it to shreds with
                    his teeth!

                              OWEN
                         (dumb-founded)
                    With his teeth!...

The men look at each other, terrified, as we -

                                             FADE OUT:

FADE IN:

62   EXT. - BLACK FOREST - WIDE - NIGHT - (STOCK)

A landscape of dark woods and tree-covered hills.

                                             DISSOLVE TO:

63   EXT. - A GYPSY CAMP IN THE WOODS - LONG - DAWN

Tents line the edge of the forest. A campfire is
burning out. A few carriages and wagons are standing about - also a bear-cage on wheels. Horses
are tied to the trees. Everybody is still asleep
in the gypsy camp.

64   MED. CLOSE - DAWN - CAMERA IN FRONT OF LOW FIRE

As the rising sun gradually lights the scene, the
horses suddenly begin to NEIGH and move about;
the dogs begin to BARK. Then into the PICTURE
steps a tall man - Larry. He stops in front of the
fire.

65   CLOSE ON LARRY - AND ERNO

The reflection of the dying flames casts wierd
shadows over Larry's white face. His hair hangs
over his forehead; his hands are dug deep into the
pockets of his long overcoat.
Into the SCENE walks Erno, an old gypsy. He stops
near Larry and looks into his face. Having never
seen this stranger before, he asks:

                    ERNO
          What do you want here,
          at the break of day?

                    LARRY
                 (woodenly)
          I'm looking for an old woman -
          her name is Maleva...
          Is she here with you?

                    ERNO
          Maleva? Yes, she is with us -

                    LARRY
                 (in sudden
                 excitement)
          Lead me to her - quick!

Erno points toward a tent and says:

                    ERNO
          You'll find her over there...

He looks after the stranger with an expression of
distaste, as Larry strides out of the PICTURE.

66   INT. MALEVA'S TENT - MED. CLOSE - EARLY MORNING

Maleva, the old gypsy woman, rises to her feet as
Larry enters. She is very old and her lined face
wears an expression of shock and fear as she recognizes him.

(The tent is sparsely furnished with a bed of straw,
a few hand-woven rugs, a crude chair or two, and an
oil-lamp.)

                    LARRY
               (mutters in a
                hoarse voice)
          Maleva...

He does not make a move toward her, but begins to
sway on his feet, as if his strength was leaving him.
Maleva decides at once that she doesn't want to have
anything to do with him. Holding the tent-flap open,
she says firmly:

                    MALEVA
          Get out of here -

But Larry does not move, just looks at her piteously:

                    MALEVA (cont'd)
          Go away! And don't cross
          my path again...

She tries to whip herself into a rage and ignore his
pitiful condition. Larry starts toward the exit -
then stops and pleads:

                    LARRY
          I've looked for you all over
          Europe - hunted from town to
          town... Now I've found you -
          you can't send me away -
          I need you!

Maleva drops her hands and the tent closes behind her:

                    MALEVA
               (sadly,
                hopelessly)
          What do you want from me?

67   INT. MALEVA'S TENT - CLOSE TWO SHOT

Larry drops the coat he is wearing. He opens his
shirt and shows her the scar on his chest - the
five-pointed star - the pentagram:

>   LARRY
> You see - I still carry the
> mark of the pentagram - the
> bite of the werewolf... You
> know the curse of my terrible
> Fate...

>   MALEVA
> I cannot help you...

Larry sinks down on a chair, his head low on his
chest, as he says:

>   LARRY
> I am a human being, Maleva!
> I know love - and honor -
> and pity - like other human
> beings... But then -

He looks up at her, his face desperate, mad, terrifying:

>   LARRY (cont'd)
> I kill people! - when the
> moon is full - I change
> into a wolf -

>   MALEVA
> It is not in my power to
> help you... I have not the
> wisdom -

>   LARRY
>   (pleading)
> But you are the only one who
> understands what has happened
> to me! Nobody else believes me!
> Only you - you know. Your own
> son, Bela, was a werewolf, too.
> He attacked me - he changed me
> into a werewolf - he brought this
> curse upon me...

CONTINUED

67   CONTINUED:

A shadow crosses Maleva's face, the memory of an
old grief, as her son's name is mentioned. She
nods, deeply touched. Larry continues, urgently:

                    LARRY (cont'd)
          You watched over him until
          he was permitted to die!
          I too want to die! My life
          is a torment - to myself and
          everybody! Help me to find
          release...

                    MALEVA
                 (struggling with
                  her emotions)
          I can't...

Then she approaches him, takes his head in her hands,
lifts it up and says:

                    MALEVA (cont'd)
          But I will guard you and
          take care of you, as I took
          care of my own son...

STEPS APPROACH from outside, and the leader of the
gypsy tribe, Erno, enters the tent.

68   INT. TENT - MED. CLOSE - ANOTHER ANGLE

Erno stops, staring at Larry. His eyes wander to
the sign on Larry's chest. In panic, he turns to
run out again, but Maleva holds him back:

                    MALEVA
          Erno - don't go -

Erno turns and points to Larry fearfully, about to
question Maleva - but she breaks in swiftly:

                    MALEVA
          I must leave you, Erno -
          I must go with him -

                    ERNO
                 (shocked)
          Leave us - and go with him -
          him with that sign of the
          beast on him?

CONTINUED

68   CONTINUED:

                    MALEVA
           He is dangerous only when the
           moon is full... Then - when the
           his hour comes - when the evil
           spell has him in its grip -
           I shall watch over him...

                    FRNO
                 (bitterly)
           He will murder you!

                    MALEVA
           No... I shall take him to
           a place I know -

                    LARRY
               (with sudden hope)
        Where?

                    MALEVA
                 (to Larry)
           I know a man who has the
           power to help you...

                    LARRY
                 (eagerly)
           Help me? Who?

69   CLOSE ON MALEVA.

as she does not answer but just smiles faintly,
mysteriously...

                                  DISSOLVE TO:

70   EXT. - COUNTRYSIDE - MED. FULL - <u>DAY</u> - <u>FOG</u>

A small carriage comes down the road, with Maleva
and Larry on the driver's seat. Maleva has the
reins in her old hands. The horse pushes through
the low fog swirling around them...

                                  DISSOLVE TO:

71   EXT. - A HILLY LANDSCAPE - DAY

The carriage with Maleva and Larry drives through...

DISSOLVE TO:

72   EXT. - ANOTHER COUNTRY LOCATION - DAY

The carriage drives through. A town can be seen
in b.g....

DISSOLVE TO:

73   EXT. - NEAR VASARIA - LONG - DAY

A small town in the Bohemian Alps - "Vasaria" -
in the b.g., surrounded by a dark forest. The
carriage drives through...

DISSOLVE TO:

74   EXT. - EDGE OF THE FOREST - MED. CLOSE - LATE AFTERNOON

Outside the town, at the edge of the woods, the
carriage with Maleva and Larry comes to a stop.
They look in the direction of the town -

75   EXT. - TOWN OF VASARIA - MED. LONG

The outline of the town can be seen clearly against
the transparent sky. A medieval tower points its
Gothic structure toward the clouds. At its feet,
small houses crouch, like sheep at the feet of the
shepherd. The church bell rings for vespers; the
chimes play the old hymn "Ueb Immer Treu Und Redlichkeit" ...

76   EXT. - EDGE OF FOREST - MED. CLOSE ON CARRIAGE

with Maleva and Larry.

                    LARRY
                  (tensely)
          Is that the town?

CONTINUED

76   CONTINUED:

                              MALEVA
                    Yes - that is Vasaria...

Larry takes the reins impatiently:

                              LARRY
                    Then let's go -- what are
                    we stopping for?

As he urges the horse forward quickly -

                                        DISSOLVE TO:

77   EXT. - MAIN STREET OF VASARIA - MED. CLOSE - LATE
      AFTERNOON

      The carriage stops in front of the inn. Larry jumps
      down and helps Maleva out of the driver's seat:

                              MALEVA
                    Let's ask in here...

      She turns toward the inn, Larry following her.

78   INT. - INN - MED. CLOSE

      A young girl, Margareta, the inn-keeper's daughter,
      is lighting the lamps, with a flirtatious eye on a
      young farmer who smiles at her as he drinks his
      glass of beer.

      VAZEC, the landlord, a man with a stomach like a
      beer-barrel, is polishing glasses behind the bar.

      The door opens and Maleva enters, Larry behind her.
      Vazec looks up from his work and says rudely:

                              VAZEC
                    Go away. No beggars
                    allowed here.

      But Maleva steps closer to the counter. The young
      girl stares at Larry, fascinated by his strange
      gaunt appearance. He turns and gives her a long
      look - and she retreats, visibly frightened.

                                        CONTINUED

78   CONTINUED:

Maleva speaks to the landlord:

                    MALEVA
          We just want to ask you, sir,
          about a Doctor Frankenstein -

The landlord looks at her unpleasantly:

                    VAZEC
          Frankenstein!
                    (with a short
                     sharp laugh)
          Don't mention that name
          around this town!

                    LARRY
                    (wildly)
          But won't you tell us
          where he lives?

The landlord puts down the glass he has just polished
and pointing his thick finger toward the window, says:

                    VAZEC
          There...

Larry and Maleva turn and look -

79   THROUGH WINDOW OF INN - LONG - (MINIATURE)

Through the window, a ruin can be seen, standing at
the top of a hill. Behind it the towering mountains,
snow-covered, veil their pointed crests in gray clouds.
Only a few walls and broken arches - the skeleton of
a strong tower - are left. The walls are fire-
blackened, desolate, forbidding...

(Above the ruins, a water reservoir, a dam and sluice-
gates can be seen.)

                    VAZEC'S VOICE
          That's his burial-place!
          The fire destroyed him
          and all his misdeeds!

80   INT. INN - MED. CLOSE - THE GROUP

Maleva and Larry turn back to the landlord from
the window:

                    MALEVA
                (shocked, sad)
            He's dead?...

Larry cries out:

                    LARRY
                (stricken)
            It can't be true!

Vazec laughs derisively and picks up another glass
to polish - while Margareta continues to watch the
strangers:

                    VAZEC
            He didn't die any too soon
            for us... We all wish he'd
            never been born!
                (then, with
                 sudden suspicion)
            What did you want from him?

He looks threateningly at the old gypsy woman and
the tall stranger:

                    MALEVA
            I heard he was a great doctor
            who could help people that
            other doctors could not cure -

                    VAZEC
            Him? Murder and all sorts of
            crimes was all he brought us!
            He harboured a monster in his
            house - a thing created by
            black magic!

                    LARRY
                (to himself,
                 in despair)
            Dr. Frankenstein is dead...

                    VAZEC
            Yes - and his bones were buried
            in the corner of the graveyard
            where the bad people lie...

CONTINUED

80   CONTINUED:

> VAZEC (cont'd)
> - the ones who do away with
> themselves and die without the
> blessing of the Church... He
> wasn't even worth that honor -

Maleva bows and says:

> MALEVA
> (gravely)
> I thank you, sir, for the
> information...

She turns toward the door. But Larry stands rooted
to the spot, staring at the landlord. Vazec comes
out from behind the bar, a glass in his hands, and
shouts at Larry:

> VAZEC
> Get out of here - and stay
> out - you and all your kind -
> tramps and sooth-sayers!
> We want to live in peace and
> quiet - we don't want any
> strangers around -

While he is speaking, Maleva turns back, takes
Larry's arm and hurries him out. Vazec slams the
door behind them. He turns angrily - the glass
crashes from his hand on to the floor and breaks:

> VAZEC
> (angrily)
> You see? They just look at
> you - and you have bad luck...

Margareta looks after the strangers and shudders
with superstitious fear...

DISSOLVE TO:

81   EXT. - COUNTRY ROAD - <u>EVENING</u> - (PROCESS)

From a pole slung behind the driver's seat, an oil-
lamp swings, throwing a lambent light on Larry and
Maleva on the seat of the carriage. The tired horse
moves along slowly. Larry stares in front of him,
then says:

CONTINUED

81   CONTINUED:

                                    LARRY
                                  (bitterly)
                        There's no hope in my living -
                        and no longer any hope that
                        I can die...

        Maleva, holding the reins in her weak hands, looks
        at him with a pity too deep for words. She turns
        her head toward the sky. Behind them the snow-
        covered mountain peaks look down like the ghosts
        of mute giants wrapped in shrouds.

82   EXT. - THE MOUNTAIN-TOPS AND THE SKY - LONG - <u>EVENING</u>

        The sky becomes lighter as the moon, still hidden
        behind the mountains, ascends.

83   EXT. - THE CARRIAGE WITH LARRY AND MALEVA - MED.
        CLOSE - (PROCESS)

        Larry, as if impelled against his will, mechanic-
        ally turns his head toward the mountains where the
        moon is rising.

84   EXT. - SKY AND MOUNTAINS - LONG - <u>NIGHT</u> - (MINIATURE)

        The lifeless disk of the moon climbs over the edge
        of the mountains and sends its pale light down into
        the dark valley. Suddenly the ruins of Franken-
        stein's house appear clearly visible.

85   EXT. - ROAD - MALEVA AND LARRY - MED. CLOSE - <u>NIGHT</u>
        - (PROCESS)

        Maleva and Larry on the moving carriage seat.
        Maleva, with a frightened half-turn of her head,
        looks at Larry's hands. Larry too looks down at
        them, his face in agony and desperation.

86   CLOSE - LARRY'S HANDS - (TRICK SHOT)

        The fingers seem to swell and bend - the nails grow
        into claws - and a thick growth of hair begins to
        sprout on the back of the hands.

87   EXT. - ROAD - MED. CLOSE - FEATURING LARRY -
      NIGHT - (PROCESS)

      He stares at his hands - an expression of boundless
      horror transfixes his features. He looks at Maleva
      - then back to his hairy claws again - in utter dis-
      may. Suddenly, without a word, he jumps from the
      carriage.

88   EXT. - ROAD - ANOTHER ANGLE - MED. CLOSE - MALEVA

      As she controls her fear, pulls the horse to a stop
      and cries out:

                         MALEVA
            Wait! - Come back!

                       MED.
89   EXT. - ROAD -/LONG - NIGHT

      But Larry, like a moving shadow, pays no attention
      to Maleva's call - only runs fast and wolfishly
      towards the ruins of the Frankenstein sanitarium.
      Soon he disappears - the night swallows him up.

90   EXT. - MALEVA - MED. CLOSE - NIGHT

      The bright light of the moon paints clear shadows
      of Maleva and the horse on the yellow road. She
      clambers down from the seat of the carriage as fast
      as her old legs can carry her and looks toward where
      Larry ran away (FACING CAMERA), crying out:

                         MALEVA
            Stop! Don't go - don't...

      But as there is no reply, she sets out on foot to
      look for him...

                                          DISSOLVE TO:

91   EXT. - SKY - FULL MOON - NIGHT

      The full moon, yellow and enormous, glares from the
      cloudless sky.

92   EXT. - VASARIA - LONG - NIGHT

The moon throws its bright light on Vasaria.
The streets of the town seem deserted at this hour.
Now the silence is broken by the eerie CRY OF A WOLF,
which ululates through the night - once - twice...
The dogs of the town wake up and answer the animal
cry with their FURIOUS BARKING.

93   EXT. - HILL-TOP - MED. LONG - NIGHT

At the top of a small hill sits a wolf, HOWLING.

                                        DISSOLVE TO:

94   EXT. - HILL-TOP - MED. CLOSE - HEAD OF THE WOLF -
      NIGHT

as he raises it toward the sky, HOWLING...
From afar, the BARKING DOGS answer him.

95   EXT. - SKY - THE MOON - LONG - NIGHT

Clouds race toward the moon and extinguish its light.
At the same time, the HOWLING of the WOLF and the
DOGS' FURIOUS BARKING dies away...

                                        DISSOLVE TO:

                                    MED.
96   EXT. - MAIN STREET IN VASARIA -/LONG - NIGHT

CAMERA HOLDS on the picture of the small, low-gabled
houses and deserted streets...
Now a crowd is approaching - it can be HEARD,
MURMURING, LOUDER NOW... Footsteps come closer and
the diffused light of oil-lamps shines around the
farthest corner in b.g.
CAMERA DOLLIES along the street, as the crowd appears
from around the corner.
In front of the people walks Vazec, the landlord of
the inn. In his arms he carries the inert body of
a young girl, his daughter Margarita, whose arms
and feet dangle lifelessly.

                                        CONTINUED

96   CONTINUED:

CAMERA COMES CLOSER, meeting the people half-way,
FOCUSSING on the stern face of Vazec, frozen in
grief and terror.

CAMERA STOPS IN MED. CLOSE: Vazec arrests his
steps and turns, bewildered. Then he moves to the
left, toward his inn, and disappears inside, followed by a few of the people.

97 ·   EXT. - OUTSIDE THE INN - MED. CLOSE - THE CROWD -
NIGHT

Frightened and upset, the people huddle together,
their oil-lamps lighting the scene. Some are holding dogs on leashes.
Franzec, the blacksmith, asks in a faltering voice:

                    FRANZEC
            Who do you suppose did
            this terrible thing?

Rudi, the tailor, replies hoarsely:

                    RUDI
            Could it be the Monster again -
            Frankenstein's monster?

                    FRANZEC
            No! The Monster burned to
            death with Doctor Frankenstein!
            We found its bones - and
            buried them -

Varja, a young woman, interjects:

                    VARJA
            How do you know they were
            the Monster's bones?

Now Cuno, the policeman, speaks up:

                    CUNO
            She wasn't killed by the
            Monster. An animal bit her
            to death - I saw the wound
            on her throat -

                                        CONTINUED

97   CONTINUED:

                              RUDI
                          (heatedly)
                    What animals are around here
                    that can kill people?

Suddenly a deep silence falls over the crowd, as
the wailing HOWL of a WOLF comes from the hills
again. The dogs answer, BARKING WILDLY, and try
to break away from their leashes.

98   EXT. - OUTSIDE THE INN - ANOTHER ANGLE - NIGHT

Cuno, the policeman, looks at his howling dog,
eager to break away:

                              CUNO
                    A wolf! -

The wolf's HOWLING is repeated, a triumphant,
blood-curdling cry:

                              RUDI
                    Yes - a wolf! That's
                    his cry -

                              CUNO
                    Come on - let's get him!

His barking, excited dog pulling him on, Cuno starts
out and the other men run after him.

99   EXT. - MAIN STREET - MED. LONG - NIGHT

As the men, brandishing their weapons and swinging
their lamps, run toward the hill with their dogs,
Cuno in the lead. From the hill-top comes again
the eerie CRY OF THE WOLF...

100   EXT. - HILL-TOP NEAR RUINS OF FRANKENSTEIN SANITARIUM -
       LONG - NIGHT

From afar we see the excited crowd running up the
hill, illuminated by their oil-lamps.
Suddenly SHOTS ARE FIRED, and a VOICE CRIES OUT:

                                        CONTINUED

100   CONTINUED:

                                    RUDI'S VOICE
              There he is! -

101   EXT. - HILL-TOP - MED. CLOSE - NIGHT

        Cuno and his barking, excited, but at the same
        time frightened dog look toward the CAMERA. Be-
        hind Cuno stands Rudi. He FIRES HIS SHOTGUN.
        The dog, barking runs toward CAMERA.

102   EXT. - HILL-TOP - MED. CLOSE ON HUGE ROCKS - NIGHT

        Behind the gigantic moraines, or rocks left in the
        wake of a glacier, the wolf-man runs - so swiftly
        that his ungainly body passes by like a shadow. -

103   EXT. - HILL-TOP - (SAME AS 102) - MED. CLOSE - NIGHT

        Cuno raises his gun and FIRES o.s. at the wolf-man.
        Other men have run into PICTURE behind Cuno and Rudi.

104   EXT. - ROCKS - (SAME AS 105) - MED. CLOSE - NIGHT

        The wolf-man rears, hit by Cuno's shot. Then he
        turns and runs.

105   EXT. - HILL-TOP - CLOSER TO RUINS - MED. LONG - NIGHT

        The wolf-man runs into the PICTURE, looking back and
        panting like a hunted beast. CLOSER comes the NOISE
        of his pursuing enemies. The wolf-man lifts up a
        rock and sends it crashing down the hill toward his
        pursuers.

106   EXT. - HILL-SIDE - NEAR RUINS - MED. LONG - NIGHT

        The men are running up the hill toward the ruins of
        the Frankenstein Sanitarium. Rocks, hurled by the
        wolf-man above (o.s.) are crashing down toward the
        men, leaping and flying, bouncing up from the ground
        and as they fall again, scattering more rocks, like
        an avalanche.

107   EXT. - HILL-SIDE - MED. CLOSE - <u>NIGHT</u>

One of the men is hurt by the falling rocks, and his lamp smashed. The burning oil flares like a bonfire. The other villagers pay no attention to him but keep on running up toward the wolf-man (c.s.)

108   EXT. - THE RUINS - MED. CLOSE - <u>NIGHT</u>

The wolf-man pushes a crumbling wall with all his might. The structure collapses, rolling down-hill toward the men below, disintegrating on its way.

109   EXT. - HILL-SIDE - LONG - DOWN SHOT - <u>NIGHT</u>

Part of the ruined wall crashing down toward the men, as hurled by the wolf-man above (o.s.) But the men keep charging up the hill to get him, firing their guns as they run.

110   EXT. - THE RUINS - MED. CLOSE - <u>NIGHT</u>

(Same as 109). The men arrive - but the wolf-man has disappeared, as if the ground had swallowed him. The men search around -

MEN'S SHOUTS
(ad lib)
Where is he? -
It was here a minute ago -
Look out - it might jump
out at you! -

More men enter the scene and look around - but no trace of the wolf-man can be found.

111   INT. CATACOMBS - LONG - <u>NIGHT</u>

This is part of the cellars, tunnels and corridors over which the medieval house had been built, used by Dr. Frankenstein as a sanitarium.
In Springtime, the melting ice sends a crushing stream of grey water through these catacombs, carrying rocks, logs, brush and dead animals, on its way downhill.
In Summer, the stream dries up, littering the stony ground with debris, which lies there until it is swept on again by the new floods of the next year.

CONTINUED

111   CONTINUED:

Now it is still Winter - the white tentacles of a
glacier fill a part of the catacombs with transparent solid ice, waiting to be melted by the
Spring sun.

On the left are man-made walls and stone arches;
to the right, the ice of the glacier; and on the
ground, the refuse of the dried-up stream.

Along this corridor runs the wolf-man. Diffused
lights, seemingly from nowhere, shine through the
tunnel from holes in the roofing.

Before the beast reaches the CAMERA, it stops,
turns, exhausted, then slowly sinks to its knees.
As it collapses -

                                        DISSOLVE TO:

112   EXT. - SKY AND MOUNTAINS - LONG - <u>NIGHT</u> - (STOCK)

The moon is just disappearing, fading away in the
first light of the new day.

                                        DISSOLVE TO:

113   EXT. - HILL-SIDE - MED. CLOSE - <u>DAWN</u>

The men, still searching between the rocks, look
strained and weary in the pale light of breaking
day. The dogs are running around in circles, unable to pick up the scent of the wolf-man.

Suddenly a voice shouts:

                    FRANZEC'S VOICE
          Here! Come here - quick!

The men turn and run to the right, where the voice
comes from, and the dogs bark wildly.

114   EXT. - ANOTHER HILL-SIDE LOCATION - MED. CLOSE -
        DAWN

        The men, brandishing their weapons, pass the CAMERA
        (which then PANS with them).
        Suddenly we see - not the wolf-man - but Maleva,
        frightened, cornered by the barking dogs.
        In front of her stands Franzes. The men stop -
        some pull back their dogs:

                          RUDI
                The gypsy woman!

        Cuno walks up to Maleva and demands:

                          CUNO
                What are you doing here?

        But Maleva only looks into his face and says nothing:

                          RUDI
                Come on - speak up, old witch!
                Where is that strange man
                that was with you?

        The old woman stands motionless, silent, putting
        up a brave front. Cuno thrusts his gun almost into
        her face:

                          CUNO
                Let's take her back to town -
                we'll make her talk!

        And brutally he takes Maleva's arm, pulling her along,
        while the crowd marches behind, shouting and threat-
        ening her.

                                          DISSOLVE TO:

115   INT. CATACOMB - LONG - DAY

        The light in the catacomb has changed; it is bright-
        er now, though still seeming to come from nowhere.
        The unseen sun makes the icy tentacles of the glacier
        glow.

        The constant melody of trickling water IS HEARD -
        snow melting somewhere, flowing away in a small brook
        in the middle of the cave. The approaching Spring is
        beginning to melt the glacier.

                                          CONTINUED

115   CONTINUED:

In the center of the cave, a man (Larry) - lies,
unconscious, on the ground, which is littered with
the refuse of the previous year's flood.

116   INT. CATACOMB - MED. CLOSE - DAY

Larry has changed from the wolf into human form
again, with the coming of the day. His clothes,
torn by his flight, hang in shreds from his body.

The light INCREASES, as the sun moves higher. The
small TRICKLE of water, passing through the center
of the catacomb to disappear underground, becomes
STRONGER and the icy water reaches Larry's hands
and face, pushing a small wave against his cheek.

Larry moves, opens his eyes. Fearfully he looks at
his hands - but the hairy growth has disappeared -
and he realizes that the time of his spell has
passed away once more. Slowly he sits up, looking
around, bewildered.

CAMERA PANS TO SHOW WHAT HE SEES: the icy tentacles
of the glacier, blocking the catacomb at one end -
at the other end is the stone foundation - man-built,
but without an exit now. Overhead, in the roof, a
big hole gapes; the wolf-man must have fallen down
from there into this underground cave.

CAMERA FOCUSSES ON LARRY AGAIN: he tries to find
some way out - but realizes he is trapped here like
an animal. He pushes against the walls, knocks on
the foundations, tries to reach the hole in the roof
-- all to no avail.

Frightened, he instinctively calls out, hoping against
hope that some-one may hear him:

                    LARRY
          Hullo!... Help!...

But only his own voice answers him in ECHO. He looks
around again - desperate -

117   INT. CATACOMB - NEAR GLACIER - MED. CLOSE - DAY

There, at the end of the cave, the light shines
brighter and the ice of the glacier is cracked.
Larry picks up a heavy log and hits it against the
snowy wall. Under the impact, a big lump of ice
breaks loose. Suddenly Larry stops and stares:

118   CLOSER ON BLOCK OF ICE AND MONSTER

Larry sees that a huge dark object is frozen into
the ice. Its contours are distorted, as if hidden
behind frosted glass.

119   MED. CLOSE -

Larry works feverishly, cracking up the ice with his
big log. The icy walls crumble under his blows. A
large segment of the glacier breaks loose and crashes
on the stone floor. Larry stops and stares again at
the object frozen inside the ice:

120   CLOSE ON MONSTER IN ICE

Clearer now, the contours of a huge figure are seen,
frozen in its icy grave in strange contortion, its
arms outstretched in a vain attempt to free itself
in its last struggle.

121   MED. CLOSE - LARRY AND MONSTER

Using his bare hands now, Larry again attacks the ice.
The crumbling glacier finally gives way, like an un-
hinged door. Clear now before Larry's eyes lies the
enormous, frozen form of the Frankenstein monster,
still half-buried in its transparent grave.

122   CLOSE - ANOTHER ANGLE - MONSTER AND LARRY - (DOWN
      SHOT)

The monster's ungainly head, stiff as in rigor mortis,
slowly falls back, its leathery throat stretches, its
ugly lips begin to quiver listlessly. Then it opens
its eyes, dully; they stare at Larry without compre-
hension.

.   CONTINUED

122   Astounded, Larry gazes at this phantom - then re-
        doubles his frantic efforts to free the monster
        completely from his icy prison...

                                        DISSOLVE TO:

123   INT. CATACOMB - MED. CLOSE - DAY

        The monster now sits on the stony ground, his back
        supported by the wall. Around him. Larry has built
        a couple of small fires from the driftwood in the
        cave.
        Larry sits close to the monster, watching it with
        burning eyes.
        The monster holds out weak hands toward the flames
        and moves his body forward to warm himself, at the
        same time trying to focus his vision on Larry:

                            MONSTER
                Where are you?
                I can hardly see...

        Larry pushes him back:

                            LARRY
                Watch out - you'll burn yourself...

                            MONSTER
                        (repeats, dully)
                Burn myself...?

        Then it turns its ugly head toward Larry:

                            MONSTER
                        (trying to get up)
                Help me to get up...

        Larry goes over to the giant and helps him to his
        feet.

                            MONSTER (cont'd)
                Once I had the strength of a
                hundred men... It's gone...
                I'm sick...

        He stands, with Larry's help, and supports himself
        against the wall.

124   INT. CATACOMB - ANOTHER ANGLE - DAY

MONSTER
We must find the way out...

He gropes against the wall. Larry taps the walls,
too, moving around, trying to find an exit.
CAMERA SLOWLY PANS with them. As they search, Larry
says:

LARRY
How did you get here?

MONSTER
(laboriously)
The village people wanted to
kill me - they burned the house
down - Dr. Frankenstein died before my eyes... I ran - my clothes
afire - down into the cellar -
toward the ice-house where I would
be safe... But I fell into the
mountain-stream... I lost con-
sciousness... When I woke up -

He points toward the wall of ice in horror:

MONSTER (cont'd)
I was frozen into that block
of ice - conscious for years -
unable to move!

Larry stops and looks at the monster, aghast:

LARRY
(terrified by
his memory)
B uried alive!... I know -

MONSTER
(nodding)
Yes - buried alive - until
you found me...
(turning to Larry)
Who are you?

LARRY
(hesitantly)
My name is Lawrence Talbot -

CONTINUED

124   CONTINUED:

                              MONSTER
                    What are you doing here?

                              LARRY
                    Hiding... the same as you -

                              MONSTER
                              (scornfully)
                    Those futile little mortals!
                    Do you hate them, too?

                              LARRY
                              (bitterly)
                    Yes.

                              MONSTER
                              (eagerly)
                    Then you are my friend...
                    I need friends - so do you.
                    We can help each other -

Larry looks at him grimly - then:

                              LARRY
                    But how do we get out of here?

                              MONSTER
                              (groping around
                               again, half-blind)
                    The laboratory must be behind
                    the ice -

125   INT. CATACOMB - WIDER - LARRY AND MONSTER - <u>DAY</u>

Attracted by the light which falls through the hole
in the ceiling, the monster says:

                              MONSTER
                    No! Up there! I remember now -

Larry looks up and realizes they must climb through
that hole. He begins to collect logs and drift-
wood, quickly, to build a platform beneath the hole
in the roof...

                                        DISSOLVE TO:

126   INT. CELLAR - <u>DAY</u> - LONG

This is a part of the cellar of the destroyed
Frankenstein sanitarium (as seen partially in
"The Ghost of Frankenstein"). A staircase, half-
destroyed, leads to the burned-down upper floors.
The roof of the corridor is caved-in here and there;
the walls are blackened by the devastating fire
which obliterated the upper floors.
But these cellars, where Frankenstein had installed
the instruments and machinery he used for his experiments, have survived the disaster fairly un-
damaged. Beams of light fall through some crevices,
indicating daytime.

A RUMBLING OF WOOD AND STONES comes from the end
of the cellar; a beam, hanging askew from the ceiling, is pushed aside. The dust of falling masonry
begins to fill the air - and as it settles - Larry
and the monster make their way TOWARD CAMERA.

Larry pushes the debris out of his way - the monster
follows him, half-blind, groping his way with both
hands, touching the wall.

127   INT. CELLAR - MED. CLOSE

Larry stops and turns toward a heavy door resting on
huge hinges. He pushes it open with all his might.

128   INT. - LABORATORY - LONG - <u>DAY</u>

This room also shows the devastation of the fire.
One part is caved-in, having smashed some of the
intricate machines with which Dr. Frankenstein used
to work. In one corner stands - towering - cemented
deeply into the ground - a cyclotron - an atom-
smashing machine.
The dust of years has settled over the room. Spiders
have found their way into the cave and spun their webs.
An operating table stands in the middle of the laboratory. Larry and the monster enter.

129   INT. - LABORATORY - MED. CLOSE

as Larry and the monster come in. The giant gropes
his way to the operating table, and pushing away the
debris covering it, sits down heavily, turning his
enormous face toward Larry.

CONTINUED

129   CONTINUED:

Larry steps closer and looks around:

> MONSTER
> (sadly)
> If Dr. Frankenstein were still
> alive - he would restore my
> sight... He would give me back
> the strength I once possessed -
> the strength of a hundred men...
> so that I could live forever!

Larry has walked over to the cyclotron - and he
turns now, aghast at what the monster is saying:

> LARRY
> Don't you ever want to die?

> MONSTER
> Die? Never! Dr. Frankenstein
> created this body to be immortal!
> His son gave me a new brain, a
> clever brain. I shall use it
> for the benefit of the miserable
> people who inhabit the world,
> cheating each other, killing each
> other, without a thought but their
> own petty gains. I will rule the
> world! I will live to witness the
> fruits of my wisdom for all eternity!

The monster leans back, gloating over the picture
of his brilliant future. But Larry, thinking only
of his own tragic life, asks:

> LARRY
> But if you wanted to die...?

> MONSTER
> I never think of death.
> I want to get strong and well -

> LARRY
> (intensely)
> But if you grew tired of living -
> if the light of day and the dark
> of night became unbearable to you -
> would you still cling to this earth
> through the centuries - with no
> hope of finding peace? What would
> you do if you wanted to die?

130   CLOSE TWO SHOT

Larry has walked over to the monster and looks at him,
intently, anxiously. For a moment, the monster is
stunned by this strange demand. Then he says, proudly:

                    MONSTER
          The story of my creation is
          written in Dr. Frankenstein's
          diary. He knew the secret of
          immortality - and he knew the
          secret of death!

                    LARRY
                    (eagerly)
          The secret of death! He knew it -
          Where is the book? I've got to
          have it!

The monster eyes him suspiciously with his half-blind
eyes:

                    MONSTER
                    (doubtfully)
          You?... Why should you have it?

                    LARRY
                    (persuasively)
          I need it - to help us both!
                    (seeing the monster's
                    hesitation)
          You said I was your friend...
          Who else will help you,
          if I don't?

The monster is still reluctant to trust Larry:

                    MONSTER
          How do I know you won't
          trick me?

                    LARRY
                    (shaking the monster
                    excitedly)
          You've got to trust me! The
          diary will tell how to cure you -
          how to give you back your strength -
          your eyesight. You're weak - you
          couldn't defend yourself if the
          people from Vaseria attacked you
          again -

                                        CONTINUED

130   CONTINUED:

                    MONSTER
                 (disdainfully)
              They can't kill me...

Larry desperately tries to make the monster believe
him:

                    LARRY
              But if they catch you - chain
              you and bury you alive - five
              rods deep - with tons of earth
              on your body - where would your
              power be then?

The monster looks frightened, stunned. Larry repeats, persuasively:

                    LARRY (cont'd)
              Where is that diary?

The monster gets up clumsily, walks toward the door,
groping his way:

                    MONSTER
              Come with me...

                                        CUT TO:

131   INT. - STUDY - MED. FULL - DAY

A small room adjoining the laboratory. This too
shows traces of the devastating fire which destroyed
the upper part of the old building. The walls are
blackened by smoke and portions of them have caved in.
This was the study of Dr. Frankenstein - where he
used to change his clothes and write notes on his
experiments, after his laboratory work.
An open cupboard shows several articles of his cloth-
ing, still hanging there.
Against the walls are many bookcases - piles of books
have fallen out and litter the ground. On the whole,
however, the room has suffered little damage from
the fire.

Into the scene walk the monster and Larry.

                                        CONTINUED

131   CONTINUED:

The monster gropes his way toward the bookcases,
stops at a particular section, and rips away a board
with his big hands. A hidden lock SNAPS, SQUEAKING,
- the bookcase moves on hidden hinges - and a small
hole in the wall is revealed before Larry's avid
gaze. Inside stands an iron-bound strong-box.

132   STUDY - MED. CLOSE

as the monster reaches into the hole and feels the
box:

MONSTER
Here it is -

As he takes it out, Larry snatches it from his hands
and tries to open it:

LARRY
(excitedly)
It's locked. Where's the key?

The monster looks baffled. Larry stares at him -
then suddenly turns and runs out of scene, the
precious box in his hands. The monster stands still
a moment - then moves forward clumsily:

MONSTER
Wait! Don't leave me -
wait! -

He follows Larry, afraid he's run away.

CUT BACK TO:

133   LABORATORY - MED. CLOSE

Larry stands at a work table. With hammer and chisel
he tries to pry open the box. The monster walks into
the picture and stands beside Larry:

MONSTER
I was afraid you'd run away -

But Larry pays no attention to him. With all his
strength, he presses the chisel between the upper and
lower lids of the box - and it flies open.

134   CLOSE - TWO SHOT

Larry hastily pulls papers out of the box - with
both hands. They are bank-notes. Carelessly he
throws them to the ground - picks out other papers
- letters - notes - looking at them briefly and
discarding them too:

                    LARRY
                (breathlessly)
        A diary... Are you sure this
        is where he kept it?

                    MONSTER
                (worried)
        Yes - it was a book with
        brass clasps -

Larry takes out the last contents of the box. A
picture falls to the ground. Larry does not look at
it.

                    LARRY
                (hope gone)
        It's not here...

The monster picks up the box and feels inside it
with his huge hands:

                    MONSTER
        Gone...

                    LARRY
                (in despair)
        The fire destroyed it...

The half-blind monster leans against the work-table
and says, equally lost and despairing:

                    MONSTER
        It can't be - it must not be...

Larry looks around like a hunted beast - then his
eyes fall to something on the ground -

135   CLOSE ON GROUND - THE PICTURE OF ELSA

There lies the photograph of a girl. Larry bends
down and picks it up. We see the girl's face and
the inscription written below it:

                                        CONTINUED

135   CONTINUED:

                         LARRY
                        (reading)
                "To my dear father.
                                Elsa"

136   BACK TO TWO-SHOT

Larry straightens, staring at the picture in his
hands - then turns to the monster:

                         LARRY
                Elsa...?

                         MONSTER
                Frankenstein's daughter...

                         LARRY
                        (slowly, as hope rises
                         again - and an idea)
                Did she die in the fire, too?

                         MONSTER
                No - I remember she escaped.
                She must still be alive -

                         LARRY
                Then she must know! - where
                her father hid his secret...

137   CLOSE ON THE PICTURE -

CAMERA SHOOTING OVER LARRY'S SHOULDER, as he gazes
at the picture of Elsa again, with renewed hope...

                                        DISSOLVE TO:

138   CLOSE - ELSA - MAYOR'S OFFICE - LATER AFTERNOON

ELSA FRANKENSTEIN, a girl of about 26, handsome and
elegant, sits in the Mayor's office in Vasaria.
She seems to be slightly nervous about what she has
been discussing with the Mayor...

                                        CONTINUED

138   CONTINUED:

CAMERA PULLS BACK INTO MED. CLOSE, revealing the
old office in the Town Hall of Vasaria, a place
covered with files, a gas-lamp burning in the
middle of the room.

(OFF-SCENE NOISES ARE HEARD - from outside, in the
village square, come the VOICES of many people
busy setting up tables, hanging Chinese lanterns,
building a band-stand... all the preparations
necessary for the Festival of the New Wine - which
begins this very evening.)

                    ELSA
          And this man wants to buy
          the ruins of my father's
          estate?

                    MAYOR
          Yes, that's why I asked you
          to come here, Baroness. He
          wanted me to give him your
          address. Naturally, I refused -
          following your instructions.
          But since I know you want to
          get rid of the property - and
          all the memories connected with it -

The Mayor looks at Elsa sympathetically. To hide
her emotion, Elsa takes off her gloves, puts them
in her handbag:

                    ELSA
          And this man told you his
          name is - Taylor?

                    MAYOR
          Yes - and that's all I know
          about him -
                    (looking at the clock
                     behind him, he adds)
          He said he'd be here at six...

The clock begins to STRIKE, solemnly - and with the
last stroke, the door opens. Elsa and the Mayor turn.

139   MED. CLOSE ON THE DOOR

There in the doorway stands Larry. He is well-dressed

                              CONTINUED

139   CONTINUED:

(in Dr. Frankenstein's clothes). His face is un-
naturally pale, his expression strained. He stands
there stiffly, looking at Elsa.

140   INT. MAYOR'S OFFICE - MED. CLOSE - ANOTHER ANGLE

The Mayor gets up and makes the introductions:

                    MAYOR
          Here is Mr. Taylor - the
          prospective buyer of your
          property, Baroness Frankenstein -

Elsa looks, spell-bound, at the mysterious character
who approaches her, slowly and ceremoniously:

                    LARRY
          Baroness Frankenstein -

He pauses in front of her, looking at her with in-
quisitive, burning eyes. Elsa feels uncomfortable
under his gaze. To overcome it, she speaks lightly:

                    ELSA
          Mr. Taylor - please sit down -

Larry turns toward the Mayor and says commandingly,
impatiently:

                    LARRY
          Will you leave us - please -

The Mayor, slightly vexed at Larry's attitude, bows
to Elsa:

                    MAYOR
          If you need a witness for
          the contract, I'm at your
          service, Baroness...

Elsa bows graciously - the Mayor leaves. Larry
waits until the door has closed behind him, then he
sits down. Elsa asks:

                    ELSA
          You want to buy our land
          and its appurtenances...?

                                        CONTINUED

140   CONTINUED:

Larry sits motionless a moment, staring at her.
Then, to Elsa's surprise, he answers:

> LARRY
> I wanted to meet you -

Elsa reacts, disconcerted:

> ELSA
> I don't understand, Mr.
> Taylor -

> LARRY
> (intensely)
> I didn't know where to find
> you. The Mayor refused to give
> me your address. But I knew
> you'd come here if I offered
> to buy the property...

Elsa looks at him, alarmed, but very curious. She
decides the best thing is to treat the situation
lightly and says, as if she were amused:

> ELSA
> It's certainly a most unusual
> way to make an acquaintance,
> Mr. Taylor. But now that you've
> gone to so much trouble to meet
> me - what do you want me to do?

Larry becomes restless - then bursts out with the
words which will decide his fate:

> LARRY
> I want you to give me the
> records of Dr. Frankenstein's
> experiments with life and death -
> the records of the monster's
> creation!

Elsa gets up, horrified. She never expected such
a request:

> ELSA
> My father's diary...!

CONTINUED

140   CONTINUED - (2):

Larry rises too; his face is drawn:

                    LARRY
          You MUST give it to me!

141   INT. MAYOR'S OFFICE - CLOSE TWO-SHOT

Elsa looks into Larry's eyes - and sees so much
misery and despair there, that she replies softly:

                    ELSA
          I don't have any records
          of my father's experiments -
                    (her eyes grow
                    somber)
          and if I had - I'd destroy them!
          My father was a great scientist -
          but all he created was unhappi-
          ness - terror -

But Larry shakes his head and says with desperate
urgency:

                    LARRY
          But if I had his records,
          I'd do nothing but good -
          believe me!

                    ELSA
                    (shaking her
                    head)
          Nothing but evil can come of it!

                    LARRY
          I must have them - I must find
          them --- please help me!

But Elsa steels herself against his pleading and
looks at him coldly, distantly:

                    ELSA
          I'm sorry - there's nothing
          I can do, Mr. Taylor... The
          house burned down. I have
          never set foot on that ground
          again - and never shall. That's
          all the information I can give you...

                                        CONTINUED

141   CONTINUED:

She picks up her handbag and walks toward the door,
just as it opens and the Mayor appears, as if he
had been listening.
(The NOISES from outside go on, LOUDER NOW.)

142   REVERSE ANGLE -

The Mayor in the doorway looks toward Larry with
obvious dislike, and asks Elsa:

                    MAYOR
          Did you call me, Baroness?

Elsa shakes her head, then says with a forced smile:

                    ELSA
          We decided not to go through
          with the sale, after all...

The Mayor is about to express his regrets, when
suddenly from outside the window, there is a
BURST OF MUSIC - light and gay. Elsa stands, trans-
fixed, listening a moment, then she walks to the
window.

143   THE VILLAGE SQUARE - FROM THE MAYOR'S WINDOW -
        MED. LONG - LATE AFTERNOON

The square is being decorated for the Festival of
the New Wine. On a stand, the Schrammel musicians
are tuning up their instruments. Round about are
small tables, each table set in a bower covered with
vines, so that its occupants will have some privacy
from their neighbors. The tables have no table-
cloths. Glasses will be set out later. Chinese
lanters glow, swinging in the balmy evening breeze.
A few men are sweeping the square, to prepare it
for the dance.
From a horse-drawn wagon, wine barrels are being
unloaded - enough of them to drown the population
of Vasaria in new wine.

                    MAYOR'S VOICE
          The Festival of the New
          Wine - it begins tonight...

144   INT. MAYOR'S OFFICE - MED. CLOSE

The instruments (o.s.), tuned now, BEGIN TO PLAY.
Elsa turns back from the window, a smile hovering
on her lips:

> ELSA
> Schrammel music!
> It takes me back to my
> childhood...

The Mayor is pleased and asks her cordially:

> MAYOR
> Why don't you join us to-
> night - as our guest of honor -
> Baroness? You can take the
> first train in the morning...

Elsa is undecided, then makes up her mind:

> ELSA
> Thank you, Mayor, - of course
> I'll stay -

She turns - and sees Larry. He doesn't understand
or care about their Festival; he is thinking only
of his own desperate plight. He looks so forlorn
that Elsa is suddenly moved with pity for this
tormented-looking stranger. The Mayor catches her
expression and says to Larry, formally:

> MAYOR
> I hope Mr. Taylor, too, will
> accept the invitation - on
> behalf of our community...

Larry turns and looks at him and Elsa with dead eyes.
But then - as if a new idea had entered his mind,
he says:

> LARRY
> Thank you - I'll be there...

DISSOLVE TO:

145   EXT. - VILLAGE SQUARE - FESTIVAL - LONG - NIGHT

It is a few hours later. The people of Vasaria and
the surrounding villages are crowding the square,
in rustic scenes such as Breughel would paint.

They fill the small booths at the edge of the square.
As is customary, they have brought their own food -
hams, geese, large loaves of bread... Some people
are dancing to the tunes of the Schrammel orchestra...
Others mob the stand where Vazec, the inn-keeper and
his helpers, pour wine into thick glasses - a river
of wine to wet the thirsty throats... Happy VOICES
are shouting above the crude MUSIC, and laughter
fills the air... Boys hold their girls in their arms
inside the wine-draped bowers... Here two drunks
begin to quarrel and their neighbors interfere...
There the first victims of Bacchus quietly and un-
obtrusively slide under the table...

146   FESTIVAL - MED. CLOSE - BEHIND THE ORCHESTRA

FOCUSSING ON THE SINGER, a heavy-built man, with a
wine-reddened humorous face, who is the master of
ceremonies. He sings a folk-song - then - at a
wave of his hand - the orchestra changes its tune.
The people gather round the orchestra, laughing and
amused, their wine-flushed faces looking up toward
the singer, who now begins his improvisations...

                    SINGER
          Come one and all and sing a song,
              Faro-la-faro-li!
          For life is short, but death is long,
              Faro-faro-li!
          There'll be no music in the tomb,
          So sing with joy, and down with gloom!
          Tonight the new wine is in bloom!
              Faro-faro-li!

CAMERA DOLLIES with the singer, who steps down from
the stand now, followed by the violinist only (the
bull-fiddle, the zither, and the guitar stay behind).
The singer improvises stanzas to the fixed melody,
with which the crowd is all familiar. They all
join in on the refrain: Faro-la-faro-li, etc.
(MUSIC DEPARTMENT - PLEASE CHECK)

147   EXT. - THE WINE STAND - VAZEC AND THE SINGER -
        MED. CLOSE

Vazec is surrounded by pitchers of wine and scores
of glasses, which he has been filling. The singer
grabs a glass and slaps Vazec on the tummy. Vazec
beams:

                    SINGER
                (raising the glass)
            Tonight we toast our happy host,
              Faro-la-faro-li,
            For he's the man we love the most!
              Faro-faro-li!
                    (poking Vazec
                    in the stomach)
            He's barrel-bellied, dipper-lipped -
            For drinking wine he's well equipped.
            But where's his chest? It must have slipped!
              Faro-faro-li...

Vazec holds his fat stomach in pleased confusion.
The crowd laughs. The singer tosses off the wine
and moves on to a booth.

CAMERA MOVES ON with the singer.

Here Franzec sits with his wife. Franzec is very
drunk - and as the singer improvises his song,
Franzec tries to get up, raising a bottle of wine
in salute - but instead, he glides under the table,
where he continues to sip from the bottle, while the
singer satirizes him:

                    SINGER
            If Franzec never drank at all,
              Faro-la-faro-li,
            He might not care for alcohol,
              Faro-faro-li.
            But since he drinks them by the score,
            He loves his bottles more and more, -
            He even likes them on the floor!
              Faro-faro-li.....

While the crowd laughs, finishing the refrain, the
CAMERA GOES ON with the singer to the next booth,
where we see another village couple, Rudi and his
pretty young wife. They are kissing each other in
a fond embrace. As the singer appears at their
booth, they break apart in embarrassment. He begins
to sing:

148   BOOTH WITH LARRY AND ELSA - MED. CLOSE

Larry and Elsa sit opposite each other at the table.
Between them stands a bottle of new wine; their
glasses are filled but untouched. We HEAR THE
SINGER'S SONG to Rudi and his wife (o.s.):

> SINGER (OS.)
> Now here's a pair of newly-weds,
>   Faro-la-faro-li,
> With love and kisses in their heads,
>   Faro-faro-li.
> Tonight there's only he and she,
> Just one and two, as you can see ---
> But very soon they may be three!
>   Faro-faro-li!

The LAUGHTER OF THE CROWD COMES OVER.

Larry stares at Elsa - but there is no emotion in
his gaze -- his thoughts are far away, pondering
upon his hopeless future.

Elsa tries to life him out of his strange mood.
She does not understand him but makes an effort to
be kind:

> ELSA
> I'm sorry if I was rude
> to you, Mr. Taylor...

Larry smiles wanly and this slight lightening of
his expression encourages the girl to continue:

> ELSA (cont'd)
> I can understand that my
> father's unhappy experiments
> attracted your interest -
> as a scientist...

> LARRY
> (tersely)
> I'm not a scientist.

Elsa looks at him with curiosity and she can't help
asking:

> ELSA
> Then - what makes you so
> interested in my father's
> work?

CONTINUED

148   CONTINUED:

Larry looks down at his hands - and hides them
suddenly, as if he were afraid the growth of wolf's
hair would reappear. With his hands hidden under
the table, he looks up toward the sky. -

149   EXT. - SKY - MOON - LONG

The waning moon is a slender scythe in the dark sky.
The time of Larry's transformation into the wolf
is not yet.

150   BACK TO MED. CLOSE - LARRY AND ELSA

She looks at him questioningly, strangely touched
by his behaviour. She senses his fear and waits
for him to explain. He looks at her, trying to find
the right words:

                    LARRY
                   (slowly)
              There's a curse on me...
              Your father's diary could
              show me how to get rid of it...

Just then, into the picture walks the singer with
the violinist.

Larry and Elsa look up, Larry controlling his annoy-
ance with this interruption - and the girl smiling
politely to hide her nervousness.

151   LARRY AND ELSA - ANOTHER ANGLE

The singer grabs Larry's glass with a flourish and,
bowing to Elsa, he empties it. Elsa smiles and
graciously hands him her glass, too. The singer
accepts it with a bow of appreciation and, raising
it in a toast, improvises a new verse for Larry and
Elsa - very politely - in contrast to the crude
manner he uses for the provincials:

                    SINGER
              The wine tonight is nobly blest,
                 Faro-la-faro-li,
              By such a lady and her guest,
                 Faro-faro-li...

                                        CONTINUED

151   CONTINUED:

>   SINGER (cont'd)
>   (urging the crowd
>   to drink with him)
>   To them a toast! Come drink with me -
>   That may they ever happy be ---
>   And may they <u>live eternally</u>!
>   Faro - fa -

He does not finish the refrain line, for Larry has
leaped from his seat, trembling, pale-faced, as if
he were about to attack the singer. He has listened
to the man impatiently and to the chorus of voices
happily repeating the refrain - but when the singer
expresses the wish that he may "live eternally" -
Larry loses control of his pent-up feelings. He is
furious.

The singer, breaking off the song, is stunned. He
drops Elsa's glass of wine. The people who had
joined in the burden of the song, suddenly become
strangely still - while the music at the end of the
square goes on a few bars, the musicians not knowing
what has happened.

Larry, looking insane in his fear and rage, shouts:

>   LARRY
>   Eternally! I don't want
>   to live eternally!

He steps forward, while the frightened singer retreats:

>   LARRY
>   Why did you say that?
>   Tell me! Why? -

152   MED. CLOSE - ANOTHER ANGLE

As the singer does not answer but just backs away
with the crowd, all of whom look at him strangely,
Larry comes back to his senses, realizing the wrong-
ness of his outbreak. He looks around at the crowd,
mortified. Suddenly he becomes rigid - he stares as
he sees:

155   MED. LONG - FROM LARRY'S ANGLE

There, among the villagers, stands Dr. Harley of
Cardiff, watching Larry with scientific calm.

154   MED. LONG - FROM DR. HARLEY'S POINT OF VIEW

Larry, over-wrought, startled by this new and un-
expected development, looks as if he wanted to
escape. Then he gets control of himself and decides
to face it out. He goes back to his table and sits
down, while Elsa continues to watch him fearfully.

The singer, used to people who act strangely under
the influence of drink, turns to the next booth,
beginning his song again, - the crowd following him
and quickly forgetting the incident.

155   MED. CLOSE - THE TABLE WITH LARRY AND ELSA

Larry has seated himself again, and says, worried
and apologetic:

                    LARRY
            I'm sorry, Baroness...

She looks at him with sympathy:

                    ELSA
            You needn't apologize,
            Mr. Taylor...

A shadow falls over the table. Larry and Elsa
look up.

156   CLOSER - THE THREE - FAVORING DR. HARLEY

It is Dr. Harley, who looks at Larry and slowly says:

                  HARLEY
           Good evening, Mr. Talbot!

The girl watches the scene with growing misgivings
and embarrassment. Larry gazes at Harley blankly:

                                CONTINUED

156   CONTINUED:

                              LARRY
                    My name is Taylor, sir -
                    you must be mistaken...

But Harley leans closer and smiles:

                              HARLEY
                    I know you by the name of
                    Talbot - Lawrence Talbot.
                    You carry your identification
                    on your forehead...

Turning to Elsa, he points to the scar below Larry's
hair-line, and adds:

                              HARLEY (cont'd)
                    Pardon my intrusion...
                    You see, I performed that
                    operation - I recognize my
                    own handiwork...

157   MED. CLOSE - ANOTHER ANGLE - THE THREE

Larry gets up - he looks into Harley's eyes -
undecided whether to confirm or deny the doctor's
statements. Harley holds Larry's gaze - like a
duelist watching his opponent... Larry suddenly gives
in. Turning to Elsa, he introduces the doctor:

                              LARRY
                    This is Doctor Harley from
                    Cardiff - Baroness Frankenstein...

Elsa, relieved at the easing of the tense situation,
replies, very lady-like and smooth:

                              ELSA
                    How do you do, Doctor Harley -
                    won't you sit down...

(The singer's VOICE COMES OVER FROM A DISTANCE NOW -
but the words of his song cannot be distinguished
any longer. The CROWD REPEATS the burden of the
SONG - the MUSIC IS PLAYING.)

                              HARLEY
                    Thank you...

                                        CONTINUED

157 CONTINUED:

He sits down near Elsa, still watching Larry...
Vazek, the inn-keeper, brings new glasses and
wine. As he puts them in front of Larry, he
scrutinizes Larry's features, trying to remember
where he saw him before; but he does not connect
Larry with the unkempt, unshaven man Maleva had
brought to his place.

Larry does not pay any attention to Vazek; he
gazes back at Harley and asks:

                    LARRY
          How do you happen to be
          here, Doctor?

                    HARLEY
               (politely)
          I've been looking for you,
          Mr. Talbot - and you were
          easy to find...

Larry looks at him wonderingly. Harley, choosing
his words carefully, so as not to give too much
away to Elsa, continues:

                    HARLEY (cont'd)
          I followed the cry of
          the wolf!...

And taking some newspaper clippings from his wallet,
he starts to read from them.
Elsa looks at the doctor with alarm; she does not
understand what he means - but she feels the under-
current of menace in Harley's voice:

                    HARLEY (cont'd)
          The newspapers told me where
          to look for you...
               (he reads)
          Fontainbleu - that's near Paris ...
          Aachen - that's at the frontier
          of Belgium... Elrad - that's in
          Bavaria... and Vasaria...

He puts the papers back - and looks at Larry
questioningly xxxsomberlyx somberly:

                    HARLEY (cont'd)
          I simply followed that trail -
          and found you...

                                        CONTINUED

157 CONTINUED: ─✓

> LARRY
> You're very clever, Doctor
> Harley...

As he looks at the doctor bitterly, the MUSIC
OFF-SCENE CHANGES TO A DANCE.

158 BAND-STAND - MED. CLOSE

The singer mounts the musicians' platform again
and starts to SING to the strains of a
"SCHWADAHUEPPERL" (a folk-dance).

159 FLASH - THE PEOPLE DANCING

as they gaily go into the folk-dance.

160 RUDI'S BOOTH - MED. CLOSE

Vazec walks over to the booth where Rudi is sitting
and beckons him silently. Rudi puts down his glass
and gets up. Vazec talks to Rudi, pointing with
his head toward Elsa's booth. Rudi nods, hesitat-
ingly - but goes out of the scene - in the direction
of Elsa's booth.

161 ELSA'S BOOTH - MED. CLOSE

Harley turns to Elsa and says, to her surprise:

> HARLEY
> Mr. Talbot is returning
> to England with me -

> LARRY
> (a threat in
> his voice)
> England? I don't think
> I'll ever go back there...

She feels very uncomfortable between the two men,
the meaning of whose words she cannot follow.
She looks up, as Rudi enters the picture.
Courteously, but with determination, Rudi approaches
Elsa. The men look at him in surprise:

CONTINUED

161   CONTINUED:

                              RUDI
                         (with a bow
                          to Elsa)
                    Will you give me the honor
                    of the next dance, Baroness?

Elsa gets up at once, glad to leave the two others:

                              ELSA
                    Of course...

Then, as the men rise, she says:

                              ELSA (cont'd)
                    At our New Wine Festival,
                    it's a man's privelege to ask
                    any girl for a dance...
                              (and adds
                               smilingly)
                    - and vice-versa...

She leaves with Rudi - both dancing out of the
picture.

162   CLOSE ON LARRY AND HARLEY

As they now talk openly - fast - and in under-
tones:

                              LARRY
                    Why have you followed me?

                              HARLEY
                    You're a murderer, Talbot!

Larry laughs sarcastically:

                              LARRY
                    Prove it!

                              HARLEY
                    You're insane at times - and
                    you know it! You're sane
                    enough now to know what you're
                    doing - why don't you let me
                    take care of you?

                                        CONTINUED

162   CONTINUED:

> LARRY
> (with a
> derisive snort)
> And you think everything would
> be all right if you put me
> in a lunatic asylum?

> HARLEY
> You know that's where you
> belong - that's the only thing
> to do!

Larry stares at Harley with hatred and disdain:

> LARRY
> That wouldn't help. I'd only
> escape again - sooner or later -

> HARLEY
> But we might cure you -
> might prevent you from -
> > (he stops, holding
> > back the words
> > "murdering again")

Larry bends forward and says with tragic emphasis:

> LARRY
> I only want to die, Harley!
> That's why I'm here. If I
> ever find peace, it will be
> here!

His voice echoes his desperation. Harley leans back,
watching Larry with the eyes of an alienist.

> LARRY (cont'd)
> You understand, Harley...
> Why don't you help me?

> HARLEY
> How?

> LARRY
> Doctor Frankenstein left a
> diary... he'd recorded the
> secret of life and death...

163   BEHIND THE BOOTH - CLOSE

Unseen by Larry and Harley, Vazec stands, listening. He suddenly remembers where he saw Larry
before. He walks away, stealthily.

164   FESTIVAL - THE DANCERS - FULL SHOT - NIGHT

The dancers, whirling around to the tunes of the
orchestra.

165   EDGE OF THE SQUARE - MED. CLOSE

A young couple - Varja and a young peasant boy -
dance into the picture. The boy stops and pulls
the girl ardently into the dark night, away from
the others.

As soon as they have disappeared, Rudi and Elsa
dance into the shot. Just then, the music STOPS.
Elsa seems to be glad of the pause. She smiles -
but tiredly.

                    ELSA
          That was fun, Rudi...

The boy looks around and as he does not see Vazec
yet and the music begins again, says:

                    RUDI
          Then one more dance...

                    ELSA
          Thank you, no - I don't want
          to monopolize you! What will
          your girl think of us?

Just then Vazec walks by - Rudi sees him - and at
once says to Elsa:

                    RUDI
          Then let me dance you back
          to your table...

He puts his arm around Elsa again and dances her
out of scene.

                              CUT TO:

166   THE BOOTH WITH LARRY AND HARLEY - CLOSE

Larry, bending forward toward the doctor, says
grimly, his voice a hoarse whisper:

                    LARRY
        Don't you understand this
        is my only chance to end
        this ghastly existence?
        If I can find out Dr. Frank-
        enstein's secret - I can break
        this curse and find peace in
        everlasting death...

                    HARLEY
        That's morbid - and you feel
        that way because you're mentally
        ill... Besides, Dr. Frankenstein's
        experiments were rather bizarre.
        Medical science never acknowledged
        them.

                    LARRY
                  (bitterly)
        Of course not! You won't ack-
        nowledge anything that isn't
        in your text-books. Why don't
        you talk to that girl - his
        daughter? She could tell you
        about things her father did -
        things you never heard of in
        your medical schools!

                    HARLEY
                  (determined)
        There's no time for this nonsense.
        The moon will be full again soon
        and you should be behind bars!...
        I'm appealing to your better
        nature, Talbot, while you can
        still think normally. Come back
        with me!
                  (then with a threat
                  in his voice)
        Or do you want me to have you
        arrested here - where I can't
        help you?

CONTINUED

166   CONTINUED:

> LARRY
> (desperately)
> Isn't there anyone in the
> whole world who can understand...!

Just then, Rudi and Elsa return to the table. The
men get up politely. Elsa, smiling, her face
flushed from the dance, says, as she sits down:

> ELSA
> Why don't you dance -
> and why those serious faces?

At this moment, a CRY OF TERROR AND DESPAIR COMES
THROUGH THE NIGHT:

> VARJA (O.S.)
> Help... Help...!

Faintly the cry is heard above the music and the
noise of the crowd. Rudi, Elsa, Larry and Harley
hear it - they turn in the direction of the desperate voice. -

167   FESTIVAL - FULL SHOT

As the cry is repeated - some people stop dancing.
The MUSIC STOPS too. A deadly silence settles over
the crowd:

> VARJA AND THE YOUNG MAN (O.S.)
> The Monster!... The Monster!

168   PART OF THE SQUARE - MED. CLOSE

Varja and the young man come rushing into the scene,
in terror, breathless, crying out:

> VARJA AND THE YOUNG MAN
>
> The Monster!... The Monster!

Varja nearly breaks down, as she reaches the people
and safety. There is a MURMURING of HORROR from the
crowd.

169   THE VILLAGE SQUARE - LONG - <u>NIGHT</u>

Toward the square - out of the night - walks the
Monster, half-blind, groping its way toward the
lights. As it comes nearer, SHOUTS ARE HEARD -

170   THE SQUARE - MED. LONG

The crowd surges back, away from the monster, in
panic and flight -

171   MED. CLOSE - NEAR LARRY'S BOOTH

Larry jumps up as he sees the monster (o.s.). He
pushes the table away - the glasses and bottles
crash to the ground. Elsa and Harley have jumped
up too - Elsa instinctively grabs Harley's arm for
protection, as Larry runs out of the picture.
Rudi rushes away in opposite direction.

172   THE SQUARE - MED. FULL

As the crowd, in panic, flees. People in booths
upset tables and chairs in their terror.

                                        QUICK CUT:

173   FRANZEC - MED. CLOSE

As he drunkenly tries to get up on his tottering
legs -

                                        CUT TO:

174   THE WINE-STAND - MED. CLOSE

A group of young people crowding in behind the bar,
hoping to find safety from the monster. Vazec, the
inn-keeper, picks up a heavy bung-hole-starter as a
weapon -

                                        CUT TO:

175   THE SQUARE - MED. CLOSE

as the monster moves heavily into the area lighted
by the Chinese lanterns.

176   OTHER PART OF SQUARE - MED. FULL

where the people are running in headlong flight.

177   NEAR MONSTER - MED. CLOSE

Larry has reached the monster. He finds himself
close to a horse-drawn truck which has brought the
wine-barrels to the square.
Larry grabs the monster's arm and pulls him toward
the truck, crying out:

                    LARRY
            Here - come with me - quick!

The monster recognizes him - it's Larry he was
looking for - and with a smile on his ungainly
face, he turns clumsily. Larry pushes him toward
the truck -

178   THE SQUARE - MED. CLOSE

Some men - including the Mayor - Rudi and others -
are grabbing weapons - whatever they can pick up -
heavy sticks of wood - pitch-forks - chairs -
organizing themselves to attack the monster.
Vazec runs in to join them, with his bung-starter.

179   THE SQUARE - FULL SHOT

Some of the people are in full flight. The men in
above scene rush toward the monster - just as Larry
is pushing him onto the truck and climbing up himself -

180   THE TRUCK - MED. CLOSE

Larry, jumping on the driver's seat, grabs the reins,
whips the heavy brewery horses into a gallop, and
drives with the monster toward the hills.

181   EXT. - THE MOVING TRUCK - NIGHT

The wildly careening truck is seen from the rear
as Larry drives it toward the hills with the monster.
Some of the barrels bounce off the truck, crashing
to the ground, a danger to the pursuers who are
running after the truck - but have to stop now -
to protect themselves.

182   REVERSE ANGLE

The truck with the monster - Larry driving the
frightened horses to greater speed - disappears into
the night - while the men, brandishing their weapons,
try to run after it, impeded by the falling barrels...

                                        DISSOLVE TO:

183   INT. INN - MED. FULL - NIGHT

The inn is jammed with villagers, men and women,
who have sobered up, their high festival spirits
changed to fright and forboding.

A wild discussion is going on - no word can be understood - but it is clear that the reappearance of the
monster is what they are talking about.

184   INN - MED. CLOSE

The door opens and some men enter - the returning
posse of villagers who had tried to pursue the
monster. They are tired and downcast by the failure
of their search.
At once the voices die down - the villagers stare at
the newcomers dejectedly.

185   ANOTHER ANGLE - MED. CLOSE - NEAR BAR

As the men wordlessly take their seats, putting
down their weapons, the Mayor, who led the posse,
speaks:

                        MAYOR
            No sign of them... We must
            wait until morning...

                                        CONTINUED

185   CONTINUED:

Vazec, who has not been with the pursuers, but
stands behind his bar, selling drinks, shouts:

                         VAZEC
                It's clear to me they're
                hiding in those ruins!

Rudi, who had just sat down, jumps up angrily:

                         RUDI
                Then why don't you go up
                there and search? Do you
                know your way through those
                dark catacombs? I don't!
                Much as I want to kill the
                monster, I'd hate to crawl
                around there in the black
                of night...

Vazec shouts wildly:

                         VAZEC
                What about that Frankenstein
                girl? She can lead us -
                she's lived there!

The men and women jump up - and Franzec shouts:

                         FRANZEC
                That's right! Let's bring
                her down here!

The men storm toward the staircase which leads to
the room where Elsa is staying. But the Mayor steps
in front of them, blocking the stairs.

186   THE INN - MED. CLOSE ON STAIRCASE

The Mayor blocking it with his body, while the crowd
angrily murmurs in front of him:

                         MAYOR
                Stop! -

He lifts up his hands and commands silence:

                                        CONTINUED

186   CONTINUED:

                         MAYOR (cont'd)
               There's no need for all of you
               to storm her room - she'll come
               down if I ask her -

Vazec, who was the first to arrive at the stairs,
shouts:

                         VAZEC
               Why should we treat her so
               fancy? She's a Frankenstein!

The crowd grunts its anger toward that name. But
the Mayor says angrily to the half-drunk Vazec:

                         MAYOR
               She's a young lady who has
               done no harm to us... Stay here!

And without another word, he turns and walks up the
stairs, while the crowd stays behind, impressed by
his authority.

187   INT. - SMALL ROOM IN THE INN - MED. CLOSE - NIGHT

The room is sparsely furnished - a bed, a chair, a
bureau with an earthen wash-bowl and a jug of water.
Elsa's elegant luggage stands about...
Elsa is sitting on the only chair, while Harley
stands near the window, looking at her with sympathy.
From downstairs, the threatening NOISE of the excited
crowd, talking again, COMES OVER.

                         ELSA
                      (unhappily)
               I wish I could undo what my
               father did... I wish I could
               help these poor people...

Harley walks over to her and says with sympathetic
kindness:

                         HARLEY
               If I can be of any help...

The girl looks up with a forlorn smile, as Harley
adds:

                                        CONTINUED

187   CONTINUED: 2

                              HARLEY (cont'd)
                    Please think of me as your
                    friend...

Elsa looks at him, fighting tears, and stretches
out her hand, which Harley takes.
Just then, STEPS COME CLOSER and there is a KNOCK
on the door. They turn toward it - Elsa withdraws
her hand and calls out:

                              ELSA
                    Come in -

188   ELSA'S ROOM - MED. CLOSE ON DOOR

as the Mayor enters. He stops, looks at the girl
and says quietly:

                              MAYOR
                    The men downstairs would
                    like to talk to you, Baroness -

Elsa gets up at once and Harley steps close to her.
As she walks to the door -

                                        CUT TO:

189   THE INN - MED. FULL - NIGHT

CAMERA FOCUSSES on Vazec and crowd, from doorway.
Staircase is in b.g.
Vazec, feeling his power over the crowd, now that
the Mayor has gone upstairs, stands on a chair,
still half-drunk, a wild glow in his eyes:

                              VAZEC
                    - and that man who helped the
                    monster to escape - what is he
                    doing here? Who is he? Where
                    did he come from? -

And into the silence he tosses his answer, triumphantly:

                                        CONTINUED

189   CONTINUED:

                              VAZEC (cont'd)
                    I know this much about him -
                    that old gypsy witch brought
                    him here! - I remember very well -
                    it was the day the wolf killed
                    my poor girl!...

The crowd murmurs angrily. Cuno, the policeman,
jumps up and shouts:

                              CUNO
                    The gypsy woman's still locked
                    up in prison. Let's find out
                    what she knows about all this! -

He turns and dashes to the door, followed by Rudi.

190   MED. CLOSE - THE STAIRCASE

as Elsa and Harley, followed by the Mayor, come down.
They look with alarm at the angrily murmuring crowd.

191   FROM ELSA'S POINT OF VIEW - MED. CLOSE

The men and women look up at her, hatred in their
eyes. Vazec points at her:

                              VAZEC
                    There's the daughter of the
                    accursed Frankenstein's!

The crowd surges forward menacingly, growling.

192   THE INN - MED. FULL - NIGHT

Elsa, Harley and the Mayor in f.g. as Vazec and the
crowd press toward them angrily. Elsa turns toward
Harley helplessly, as Vazec comes closer, shouting:

                              VAZEC
                    That name has brought nothing
                    but misery and misfortune to
                    our village! We want an end
                    to it - do you hear? - tonight!

                                        CONTINUED

192   CONTINUED:

Harley steps forward and says quietly:

                    HARLEY
          The Baroness and I want nothing
          but to help you -

                    VAZEC
              (interrupting
               fiercely)

          Listen to him! He's lying!
          I heard him this evening -
          talking to that stranger about
          insanity and murder! I heard
          it with my own ears -

Harley breaks in with the authority of a doctor,
used to handle excited people. Gazing calmly at
Vazec, he says:

                    HARLEY
          Don't get excited, my good man.
          You won't get anywhere by raving -

The Mayor at once supports him:

                    MAYOR
          Doctor Harley is right. To find and
          destroy the monster, we must
          have a plan -

                    VAZEC
          But we know it's hiding in
          the Frankenstein ruins -

Elsa steps closer to Harley and says quietly:

                    ELSA
          I can lead you down there
          if you want me to - I know
          those cellars well -

But Vazec, taken aback by this spirit of co-operation,
which pushes him into the background, shouts with
hatred:

                    VAZEC
          Don't be fooled! You can't
          trust them - they're all in
          this together!

193   INN - MED. CLOSE - ANOTHER ANGLE

as the door opens and Cuno and Rudi enter, pushing
Maleva in front of them. The old woman looks weak
and tired, but a defiant fire glows in her eyes:

The people turn as she enters. Vazec points at her
and shouts toward the doctor:

                    VAZEC
          And the gypsy! She belongs
          to your gang of murderers, too!

Cuno shoves the old woman cruelly and shouts close
to her face:

                    CUNO
          Do you know these people?
          Speak up - old witch!

                    MALEVA
          I never saw them before...

Harley makes his way through the crowd, pausing before Maleva. Her gypsy dress reminds him of the
woman Larry was looking for. He asks her:

                    HARLEY
          What is your name?

                    MALEVA
          Maleva...

Harley stares at her, remembering when he last heard
her name - when Inspector Owen and he were searching
out Larry's identity in the Welsh village.

                    HARLEY
          Maleva!

Vazec pushes himself through the crowd and pointing
at the doctor, shouts:

                    VAZEC
          See - he knows her!
                    (turning to the Mayor)
          Why don't you arrest them -
          all of them? Lock them up -
          these murderers!

                                        CONTINUED

193   CONTINUED:

At once the crowd is on Vazec's side. Only a few
level-headed people stand by the Mayor, who steps
forward and says with a threat in his voice:

                    MAYOR
          As long as I am the Mayor of
          Vasaria, justice will be pre-
          served! I will decide what
          is to be done in this community!

Cuno, the policeman, steps to his side, his gun in
hand. A few others follow suit. The disgruntled
crowd suddenly becomes uneasy and silent.

The Mayor, pleased with his success in quelling the
incipient outbreak, now tries to reason with them:

                    MAYOR
          Haven't we tried before to
          get rid of the monster by
          force? We burned down the
          sanitarium - but still we
          didn't destroy Frankenstein's
          fiendish creation. We must be
          more clever this time - let's
          use our brains for once! -

Vazec, who sees he is losing ground, yells wildly:

                    VAZEC
          Whose brains? Yours? I'd
          rather depend on my fists!

But the people want to hear the Mayor's plan:

                    MAYOR
          There's no use storming the
          ruins - we must pretend to
          make friends with the monster -

                    VAZEC
                 (sarcastically)
          Why not elect it Mayor of
          Vasaria?

But as nobody listens to him, he turns and walks
away. To clinch the Mayor's hold on the people,
Harley says:

                                        CONTINUED

193   CONTINUED - (2):

HARLEY
The monster was created
artificially - it must be
destroyed by the same means -

The people indicate their assent. Elsa says:

ELSA
I'll take you to the ruins now -

HARLEY
I'll go with you, of course -
            (to the people,
            with conviction)
I promise you - if you'll only
help me - I'll rid Vasaria of
this curse once and for all!...

DISSOLVE TO:

194   INT. RUINS - UNDERGROUND STUDY - (AS IN 131) -
MED. FULL - EARLY MORNING

On the ground, propped up by pillows and covered
with blankets (found in Frankenstein's closet)
lies the monster, motionless. Only his labored
BREATHING is HEARD.
At the fireplace, Larry pushes another log onto the
flames, which throw a flickering light through the
room.
Larry has cleaned up the study as well as he could -
put the books back onto their shelves, closed the
cupboard...

195   STUDY - MED. CLOSE

Larry, at the fireplace, turns and looks at the
monster and says bitterly:

LARRY
Why did you come down to
the village? Now they'll
hunt us again -

CONTINUED

195   CONTINUED:

The monster turns his ugly face toward the fire,
beads of sweat on his forehead:

                    MONSTER
          I was afraid you'd left me -
          I thought you'd found that
          diary - and run away -

Larry gets up, walks over to the enormous, prostrate body:

                    LARRY
                  (bitterly)
          You think you're so clever -
          Frankenstein gave you a
          cunning brain, did he?
          But you're dumb! You've
          spoiled our only chance -

Suddenly he stiffens, listens, as from somewhere
outside a VOICE CALLS. The monster lifts his head -

                    HARLEY'S VOICE (O.S.)
          Talbot!... Talbot!

Larry runs to the exit - but the monster says,
fearful:

                    MONSTER
          Don't leave me - don't go!
          I'm weak... They'll catch
          me and bury me alive!...

Harley's VOICE COMES CLOSER:

                    HARLEY'S VOICE (o.s.)
          Talbot!... Where are you?

Larry stands motionless.

                    MONSTER
                  (whispers)
          Put out the fire! The smoke
          will give us away -

                              CONTINUED

195   CONTINUED: — ✓

> HARLEY'S VOICE (O.S.)
> (closer now)
> Talbot! We're here to help
> you - we can give you what
> you're looking for! Where
> are you?

Larry runs toward the exit.

196   EXT. - THE RUINS (AS IN 114) - MED. CLOSE -
EARLY MORNING

In the early dawn stands Harley, Elsa beside him;
behind them is Maleva, wrapped in her thick woolen
shawl.

> HARLEY
> (calling)
> Talbot! Come out - we're
> your friends -

Maleva points to the smoke coming out through the
ruins - the smoke of the fire Larry has kindled:

> MALEVA
> They must be there -
> where the smoke comes from -

Harley and Elsa walk over toward the direction indicated. Just then a breeze shifts the smoke - and
before them stands Larry, tall, silent, a club in
his hands.

> HARLEY
> (relieved)
> There you are!

Larry looks the group over and says gruffly:

> LARRY
> What do you want?

Elsa steps toward him:

> ELSA
> You wanted to find my father's
> diary... I'll show you where
> it is hidden -

197 EXT. - RUINS - MED. CLOSE - ANOTHER ANGLE

Larry looks at her, searchingly, and then at
Maleva, who stares at him with sad, old eyes:

      MALEVA
   She speaks the truth, my son!

Larry, after a moment's hesitation, turns and says:

      LARRY
     (hoarsely)
   I have to trust you...

They start toward the underground portions of the
ruin -

198 INT. - UNDERGROUND STUDY - MED. CLOSE - <u>DAY</u>

The monster, hearing steps approach, gets up,
clumsily. Grabbing a chair, he breaks off one of
its legs as if it were a match. Holding the chair-
leg as a club, he looks toward the door.

199 STUDY - REVERSE ANGLE

Larry, followed by Harley and the two women, enters.
Larry sees the monster's threatening attitude and
says sharply:

      LARRY
   Take it easy!

      MONSTER
   Oh, it's you...

Larry walks over to the monster and takes the piece
of wood away from him, throws it into the fire.
The monster stares toward the others, half-blind,
wondering who they are.
Elsa has stopped near the door. She cannot suppress
her horror - dreadful memories come back to her as
she sees once more her father's creation. Maleva,
nearby, consolingly puts her hand on the girl's arm.
But Harley, after having overcome his first shock,
boldly walks over to the monster.

200   STUDY - MED. CLOSE - NEAR MONSTER

The monster looks at Harley with suspicion, ready
to fight. Larry speaks sharply again:

                    LARRY
            This is Doctor Harley -
            he has come to help you -
            to make you well...

The monster slowly bends down to look at Harley
with his half-blind eyes:

                    MONSTER
                  (hopefully)
            To make me well - to give
            me back the strength of a
            hundred men?

Harley, who now gets a close look at the man-made
apparition, cannot hide his amazement.

201   STUDY - CLOSER

                    HARLEY
                (lying to Monster,
                 according to his plan)
            Yes - that's why I'm here... .

But as he gazes at the giant, it is clear that Dr.
Harley is fascinated by this phenomenon - his
scientific curiosity is unleashed. He takes the
monster's arm, pushing up the sleeve of the burned,
torn clothes, and stares at it wonderingly - this
arm put together from parts of human bodies - the
stitches of the surgeon's needle still plainly
visible. Then Harley looks at the monster's face,
gently moving the ugly head and touching the steel
bar which runs straight through the giant's throat.

                    MONSTER
            It's my eyes - I can scarcely
            see...

Harley starts to examine the monster's eyes.

202   CLOSE ON ELSA - MALEVA NEARBY

Elsa looks toward the doctor, watching him with
growing apprehension. CAMERA PANS as she walks
over to him and says in a soft voice:

                    ELSA
          Doctor Harley!

The monster moves his face toward her, listening.
Harley, realizing he has shown too much interest in
the monster, controls himself at once and turns:

                    HARLEY
          Yes...?

He sees the girl's perplexed, pleading expression.
Just then, Larry walks up to her and in a voice of
suppressed excitement, says:

                    LARRY
          The diary! Where is it?
          You said you know where
          your father hid it...

The girl nods and walks toward the book case.

203   STUDY - NEAR BOOK CASE - MED. CLOSE

The girl moves to the book case - just as the monster
had done in earlier scene. Larry and Harley follow
her into the shot. Larry calls out in despair:

                    LARRY
          It's not in there! I know -

The shelf moves - as it did before - showing the
empty niche where the steel box was hidden. But
now the girl presses a hidden spring - and the wall
snaps back -

204   CLOSE - ANOTHER OPENING BEHIND BOOKCASE

There - bound in strong leather and steel bands -
lies the Frankenstein diary. Larry rushes forward,
pulls the tome out of its hiding-place and says
breathlessly:

                    LARRY
          The secret of life -
          and death!...

                              DISSOLVE TO:

205   INT. - LABORATORY - FRANKENSTEIN RUINS - FULL - DAY

Same set as in 123. At a charred table sit Harley
and Elsa. Nearby sits Larry, head forward, eyes
glued on Harley's lips. In a corner, Maleva crouch-
es, draped in her thick shawl, like a mummy in its
wrappings.
Harley is bent over the book, reading, deeply absorbed
by this record of the monster's creation.

206   MED. CLOSE - HARLEY, ELSA AND LARRY

                    HARLEY
                   (reading)
         "Matter ages because it loses
          energy... This artificial body
          I have created has been charged
          with super-human power, so that
          its span of life will be ex-
          tended. Its life-time will equal
          the lives of more than a hundred
          ordinary human beings... This,
          my creation, can never perish...
          unless " -

Harley looks up - into Larry's anxious eyes - then
into Elsa's - and then he turns back to the pages:

                    HARLEY (cont'd)
                   (reading)
         "- unless its energies are drained
          off artificially - by changing
          the poles from plus to minus..."

Larry jumps up and walks over to the table:

                    LARRY
          If that's the secret of life -
          what good is it to me? I wasn't
          created artificially - I'm a
          human being - my heart pumps
          real blood! What are you going
          to do to end my life?

Harley looks at him, his eyes far away, then turns
back to the book:

                                        CONTINUED

206   CONTINUED:

                              HARLEY
                    Energy, which cannot be
                    destroyed, can be transmitted...

Larry, looking half-mad in his feverish desire to
understand, says:

                              LARRY
                    Then the energies of my body -
                    they can be drained out too!

He looks around - at the instruments nearby:

                              LARRY (cont'd)
                    Frankenstein did it -
                    with those instruments...

207   LABORATORY - NEAR INSTRUMENTS - MED. CLOSE

as Larry walks up to one of the instruments, whose
wiring was destroyed by the fire and now hangs like
spider's threads from the ceiling:

                              LARRY (cont'd)
                    The fire didn't destroy
                    the steel -

He turns a dial and says feverishly:

                              LARRY (cont'd)
                    They must still work -
                    why don't you make them work,
                    Harley! They'll deliver me
                    from this curse that forces
                    me to live forever!

208   LABORATORY - CLOSE TWO SHOT

Harley looks toward Larry blankly, his thoughts
far away, as if he hadn't heard Larry's plea. Then
he turns back to the book.
As Harley bends over it, Elsa's head enters the
picture. While Harley stares at a diagram, trying
to understand its meaning, Elsa watches him with
mounting alarm and suspicion:

                                        CONTINUED

208   CONTINUED:

ELSA
When you were talking to
the monster - I was afraid
you meant what you said...

Harley turns to her, his thoughts interrupted:

HARLEY
What did I say?

ELSA
You said you'd save him!

HARLEY
(abstractedly)
Of course I can't - I mustn't...
Still - to kill him...!

He sighs, troubled, then gets up.

209   MED. CLOSE

Harley steps into the middle of the laboratory and
looks up at the ceiling -

CAMERA PANS to show what Harley sees: the electric
wires - the flat and thick ones for the ampere load
- the thin ones for the high-tension - form a maze
of twisted copper.

CAMERA PANS AROUND AND DOWN TO HARLEY AGAIN - Elsa
watching him - as he says, as if to himself:

HARLEY
It shouldn't be difficult
to connect those wires again -

He walks over to the partly burned machines.

210   LABORATORY - MED. CLOSE NEAR MACHINES

as Harley steps close to an amplifier, he says:

HARLEY
I'll need these machines...
I'll have to repair them...

DISSOLVE TO:

211   EXT. - A RAILWAY RAMP AT THE VASARIA STATION - DAY

Two husky men wheel a huge wooden box toward the
CAMERA. A painted inscription on it can be read,
as the box moves into CLOSE-UP:

               "FÜR: DR. P. HARLEY,
                      VASARIA.

               FRAGILE

          VON: MASCHINEN FABRIK ULM"

The writing blots out the lens in a

                                        DISSOLVE TO:

212   VAZEC'S INN - MED. FULL - NIGHT

An oil-lamp hanging from the smoke-stained ceiling
shines on a round table where some of the respectable
citizens of Vasaria sit behind their glasses of wine.
A young girl, refilling the glasses from a pitcher
as quickly as they are emptied, circles the table.
The men are the Mayor, Rudi, Franzec, Cuno, and
Vazec, the inn-keeper.

213   INN - MED. CLOSE

Vazec's face is flushed with anger; he bangs his
big fist on the table, so that the glasses begin to
dance, and he says in a hoarse, wine-sodden voice:

                    VAZEC
               Machines! What does Harley
               need machines for? Remember
               Doctor Frankenstein - he ordered
               machines too! I tell you - that
               English doctor is no better than
               Frankenstein himself!

214   INN - AT TABLE - ANOTHER ANGLE

The Mayor looks at Vazec angrily and says:

                                        CONTINUED

214   CONTINUED:

                    MAYOR
          Always grumbling, Vazec,
          always complaining! We
          must trust the doctor -
          what else can we do?

                    RUDI
          But doesn't it strike you
          as strange that Harley and
          that Frankenstein girl never
          tell us what they're doing
          up there?

Cuno, the policeman, lights his pipe contemplatively
and puts in his opinion:

                    CUNO
          If it weren't for that old
          gypsy witch, driving her wagon
          down here now and then to buy
          their provisions, we'd never
          see any of them -- and she
          won't even answer a question!
          I think we ought to go up there
          and see for ourselves -

But the Mayor shakes his head:

                    MAYOR
          They're not harming us - it's
          none of our affair - what
          goes on there -

                    VAZEC
          Are you going to wait until
          disaster strikes us again?
          I'll tell you what we ought
          to do -

215   INN - CLOSE ON VAZEC AND THE MAYOR AT TABLE

      the other men in the b.g. Vazec dips his finger
      into the wine, and as he continues to talk, he
      illustrates his words by drawing a picture with
      his wet index finger on the wooden table.

                              CONTINUED

215   CONTINUED:

                                    VAZEC
                    Here are the ruins...
                    Down in there are - all of them...
                    Here the underground stream
                    runs - the stream that drives the
                    turbines Frankenstein installed...

216   MED. CLOSE - ANOTHER ANGLE

Vazec looks up, sees the faces of the men turn
toward him interestedly, and swollen by his import-
ance, he goes on:

                                    VAZEC
                    But the water comes from here...

He draws a line to represent the mountain, then a
line from that:

                                    VAZEC (cont'd)
                    - to the dam - here...

and lowering his voice, he adds:

                                    VAZEC (cont'd)
                    Blow up that dam - and they'll
                    all drown like rats! All of
                    them!

And with a sweep of his hand, he wipes out the wet
drawing, and looks up triumphantly. There is a
pregnant silence.

The Mayor gets up slowly and throws a coin on the
table:

                                    MAYOR
                    You're drunk, Vazec - that's
                    why I don't take your words
                    seriously -

and as he grabs his hat, he adds, threateningly:

                                    MAYOR (cont'd)
                    Otherwise, I'd arrest you for
                    conspiring to endanger the
                    lives of this community!

                                              CONTINUED

216   CONTINUED:

He looks at the other men silently, and one after
the other gets up, putting down a coin. They all
leave.

217   THE INN - CLOSE ON VAZEC

Left alone, Vazec looks after them - hatred in his
eyes...

DISSOLVE TO:

218   INT. - UNDERGROUND STUDY - MED. CLOSE - <u>NIGHT</u>

The monster, dressed by Harley in a white operating
gown, sits motionless, like a Tibetan god, leaning
his gigantic form against the wall, and watching
Larry.
Larry is pacing the floor nervously. Suddenly he
stops - as the RUMBLE of the melting ice (o.s.)
makes the floor TREMBLE.

                    LARRY
          What was that?

                    MONSTER
          The ice is melting...
          The water will be rushing
          down soon and turning the
          turbines... The machines will
          work again - and the Doctor
          will make me strong once more!

The monster gets up and steps closer to Larry.
Lifting his hands to his eyes, he says with a slow
and heavy tongue:

                    MONSTER (cont'd)
          Then I shall see again -
          and be fit to rule the world!

The RUMBLE of ice is repeated again, STRONGER NOW.

219   MED. CLOSE - ANOTHER ANGLE

The door opens and Maleva appears. She is carrying a tray of food, which she puts down on a table.
As the monster walks back to his corner, Larry
turns to Maleva:

                    LARRY
          Maleva...

The old woman turns her impassive face toward him,
as Larry stretches out his hands toward her:

                    LARRY
          can   (desperately)
          I/feel the spell beginning   -
          I don't want to live through
          that again...!

                    MALEVA
                (nodding somberly)
          The moon will be full tonight,
          my son...

                    LARRY
                (wildly)
          I can't endure it again -
          I can't!

He suddenly turns and runs out of the room, crying:

                    LARRY (cont'd)
          HARLEY!... Harley!...

The RUMBLE of the ICE COMES OVER like a distant
thunderstorm.

220   INT. - LABORATORY - MED. FULL - NIGHT

The laboratory has changed considerably. Though
still showing traces of the big fire - blackened
walls, cracked ceiling, half-burned beams, - the
instruments are now repaired, two surgery tables
stand parallel to each other, with the electrodes
attached to wires.
Harley is connecting a coil to an amplifier, when
he hears Larry calling:

                    LARRY (O.S.)
          Harley!... Harley!

He turns -

221   LABORATORY - MED. CLOSE

Larry comes running into the laboratory - just as
Elsa enters from the opposite side. Larry runs up
to the doctor, his face distorted with fear, and
cries out in agony:

                    LARRY
             Tonight - you must do it
             tonight!

222   CLOSER - ON HARLEY AND LARRY

Harley looks at Larry quietly and answers:

                  HARLEY
             I'm setting the machinery.
             You'll be all right, Talbot -
             everything will be ready for
             you in a little while...

                  LARRY
             There's so little time!
             I don't want to live through
             this night!

Elsa approaches as Harley answers Larry comfortingly,
as if he were talking to an excited patient:

                  HARLEY
             Yes, Talbot - I know...
                 (and adds
                    soothingly)
             Now I have work to do -
             you mustn't bother me...

A change comes over Larry. His excitement is replaced
by a threatening sullenness:

                  LARRY
              I warn you - it must be
             tonight!

He turns and walks stiffly out of the room.

Harley turns to Elsa. She looks after Larry with
alarm - then says to the doctor:

                                  CONTINUED

                              ELSA
                    Why don't you lock him up -
                    so you can give your full
                    attention to doing what you
                    promised - destroying the
                    danger of the monster!

Harley takes out his handkerchief and wipes his face.
He suddenly shows strain and near-exhaustion.

                              HARLEY
                    I will, Elsa - please -
                    I know what I have to do -

                              ELSA
                    But what about Talbot?
                    He's insane!

Suddenly a voice says from the corner of the room,
as Maleva enters the SCENE:

                              MALEVA
                    Insane? He's not insane...

She wraps her shawl closer around her old shoulders,
as if she felt cold:

                              MALEVA (cont'd)
                    He simply wants to die...
                    That is all he asks of
                    the Doctor -

                              ELSA
                    Are you asking Doctor Harley
                    to kill a man?

                              MALEVA
                    It would not be murder...
                    It would be an act of grace
                    to deliver this unfortunate
                    soul from the curse of such
                    suffering...

Elsa and the doctor stare at the old woman, who
continues:

                              MALEVA (cont'd)
                    My powers have failed -
                    but my prayers will be answered!

225   LABORATORY - MED. CLOSE - NIGHT

Maleva turns and walks out. Harley impatiently
goes back to his work, walking over to the switchboard, pulling a switch and watching the instruments.
Elsa watches him.

CUT TO:

224   EXT. - MOUNTAINSIDE - (MINIATURE) - NIGHT

The sluice gates, controlling the flow of water from
the dam, open slowly and a small stream of water,
increasing in volume gradually, shoots out of the
half-open gates.

CUT BACK TO:

225   INT. LABORATORY - MED. CLOSE - (ALL SCENES FROM HERE
TO END ARE NIGHT)

Harley at the switchboard. The RUMBLE of the water
increases and as Harley moves some other switches,
the electrical instruments show the increasing load.
The turbines, beginning their mournful chant,
MOUNTING TO A HIGHER PITCH, indicate the greater
power output. Electric discharges appear between the
copper poles above the instruments.

Elsa enters the shot, watching Harley with suspicion.
And for the first time, she calls his name above the
din:

ELSA
Frank!

Harley shuts off the instruments and turns:

HARLEY
(impatiently)
Yes?

He looks changed, nervous at being interrupted in
his work. But Elsa takes him by the shoulders and
turns him toward her:

CONTINUED

225   CONTINUED:

                    ELSA
          Listen to me, Frank...

Harley looks at her silently, his expression stern
and inaccessible to her pleading:

                    ELSA (cont'd)
          I saw my father become
          obsessed by his genius...
          by his power... He died a
          horrible death - just as my
          grandfather did...

                    HARLEY
                 (irritably)
          I know...

                    ELSA
          You promised you'd destroy their
          monstrous creation - you promised
          the people of Vasaria... I want
          to be sure nothing ever sways you -
          nothing whatsoever - the power of
          these secrets - nor the ghastly
          inhuman idea my grandfather conceived!
          It's in your hands to clear the
          name of Frankenstein - to undo the
          crimes my father and my grandfather
          committed!

Harley listens to her, his face gaunt and drawn.
The struggle in his heart, between good and evil,
between duty and the insatiable curiosity of the
scientist, shows in his pale features. The girl
looks at him, strong-willed, forcing him to look
into her eyes, trying to help him go the right way.

                    HARLEY
                 (hoarsely)
          All right. Tonight - I'll
          drain out the monster's artificial
          energies. And I hope i'll bring
          peace to both of them: the insane
          murderer, who wants to die -
          and the inhuman thing that wants
          to live forever...

As the girl still holds his gaze, and he bows his
head -

                                        DISSOLVE TO:

226   INT. - LABORATORY - MED. FULL

The room is bathed in strong lights. The monster,
fastened to an operating table, lies motionless in
anaesthetic sleep. The table is raised, so that the
giant is upright. Two copper connections extend from
the steel spike, which runs across his neck, to a
transformer at his right side. The giant is clad in
the white pajamas of hospital patients.

Into the room comes Harley, wheeling a similar table
on which Larry lies, also unconscious. He is clad
the same as the monster.

Harley pushes the wheeled operating table toward the
right side of the transformer.

227   MED. CLOSE

Harley bends over Larry and fastens a spike around
his neck - the same as the monster wears. Then he
connects the poles of the steel to two points on the
transformer. Then Harley turns a wheel which moves
Larry's table upright. The transformer is now in
the middle of both tables - at the left, the monster
- at the right side, Larry. Harley steps back, and
over to another table.

228   CLOSE - THE TABLE WITH FRANKENSTEIN'S DIARY

as Harley bends over the book. CAMERA BEHIND HIM,
FOCUSSING ON THE WRITING IN THE BOOK. A machine is
pictured - the same as we see between the two unconscious phantoms. The connections are drawn carefully in the picture. A figure is shown (the monster's)
and Frankenstein's clear scientific handwriting can
be read:

              "Connecting the plus-poles
               to the minus will charge
               the energy output of the
               nervous system, as by
               connecting the minus to
               the minus..."

The rest is blotted out by Harley's hand, which lies
on the book.

229   CLOSE - HARLEY - REVERSE ANGLE

He looks up, toward the monster and Larry. The
muscles of his face tighten and a mad gleam comes
into his eyes.

230   MED. CLOSE

Harley suddenly leaves the book and runs over to the
monster. He tips the table into a horizontal position.

231   CLOSE - NEAR MONSTER

As Harley, his hands trembling, hurriedly unclasps
the connections and interchanges them on the spike
at the monster's throat...

                                        DISSOLVE TO:

232   THE SLUICE GATE - LONG - (MINIATURE)

The light of the night increases as the moon climbs
up in the sky. The gate is closed - a small trickle
of water escapes through the lock of the gate.

233   MED. CLOSE - TOP OF THE SLUICE GATE

Vazec appears, climbing up on the gate. He puts a
box of dynamite hastily on the gate, and fastens a
fuse to it. He looks down toward the valley.

234   EXT. - RUINS - MED. CLOSE

Maleva puts the horse in between the shafts of her
carriage - then looks toward the sky, murmuring
anxiously, in fear of the impending disaster.

235   EXT. - MOUNTAINSIDE - (MINIATURE)

The snow-capped mountains shine brighter now, as the
moon climbs higher.

236   INT. LABORATORY - MED. FULL

Harley, at the switchboard, pulls a switch.
Behind him, Elsa enters quietly and stops, staring
at the two motionless figures on the operating tables.

237   EXT. - MOUNTAINSIDE - THE SLUICE GATES

The gates open and the water rushes through - faster
and faster.

238   LAB. - MED. FULL

BEGINNING OF THE EXPERIMENT. Harley pulls another
switch and at once the HUM of the TURBINES COMES OVER,
increasing in tension to a HIGH AND SHRILL NOTE.

239   MED. CLOSE

The instruments begin to emanate blinding flashes;
the display of lightning on the top of the transformer
joins into an electric arch.

Harley, at the switchboard, increases the output,
watching the two figures, spell-bound.

He is not aware that Elsa stands behind him, watching
him and his experiment anxiously.

Harley pulls a switchboard lever, slowly. At once
the lights of the room dim. The terrific display
of electric discharges stops. It is very quiet.

240   MED. CLOSE - THE TRANSFORMER

and the figures of the two phantoms. A strange aura
forms around Larry - a kind of halo surrounding his
whole body - an unearthly, shimmering light - which
now moves to the left - toward the monster - and
like a transparent tongue, touches the monster's head.

Larry's head slowly sinks to his chest, while the
monster becomes rigid, his ungainly head lifts up,
a new power fills his mighty chest - he opens his
eyes wide - the muscles of his big jaw stand out
like iron chains.
As Larry loses in power, the giant gains.

241   MED. CLOSE - ELSA

She stares at the transformation - she sees the
monster coming back to life!

242   CLOSE - THE MONSTER

as he stares at Elsa, an ugly smile on his lips.
Then he moves his arms, straining at the straps
that tie him to the table.

243   MED. CLOSE - HARLEY AND ELSA

He watches the experiment, spell-bound. Elsa
grabs his arm and cries out in despair:

                    ELSA
            You're making him strong again!
            You're renewing his life!

Harley does not even seem to hear her. He shakes
himself free.

                         ELSA (cont'd)
                      (desperately)
            Stop it! Stop the machines!
            Frank!

244   CLOSE - THE MONSTER AND LARRY

The monster, gaining more and more in strength,
while Larry now seems to collapse.

245   MED. CLOSE - THE MACHINERY

In a sudden move, Elsa dashes to the switchboard,
and pushing Harley's hand away, throws a lever into
contact.
There is a huge electrical discharge - a blowing of
fuses - and the switchboard begins to burn in short
sputtering bursts.
The power of the explosion rocks the room - and
shocks Harley back to reality.
He wheels - instinctively protecting the girl with
his body.
The light has gone out, but the laboratory is
illuminated by the continuous discharges of the
burning switchboard.

CONTINUED

246   CLOSE - ELSA AND HARLEY

Harley, at a loss for a moment, stares at Elsa -
then turns toward the switchboard in helpless
consternation.
But Elsa grabs his arm again and Harley follows
her mute stare:

247   MED. CLOSE - THE TRANSFORMER AND THE TWO PHANTOMS -
       (TRICK)

The monster, stunned, hangs on to his straps.
But a change comes over Larry. His face reverts
into that of the wolf-man. A hairy growth covers
his hands again. Power returns into his body,
which stiffens. He opens luminous eyes and stares
at the two people (o.s.) With a bend of his powerful arms, he breaks the straps which tie him to
the operating table.

248   MED. CLOSE - THE GROUP

Elsa cries out in terror and Harley grabs a wrench,
stepping in front of her to defend her.

The monster raises his head again. Seeing that the
wolf-man is free and is approaching the doctor, the
monster utters a hoarse cry of despair. Fighting
against the chains binding him, he tries to break
them, exerting all his strength.

249   MED. CLOSE - ANOTHER ANGLE

The wolf-man, snarling, has pried himself loose and
now attacks the doctor, who hits him with the wrench.
The phantom stumbles back, then rushes forward again,
swinging his hairy claws against his adversary.

250   MED. CLOSE - ANOTHER ANGLE

The monster succeeds in breaking the bands that hold
him. He rips away the copper wires tying him to the
transformer. Crying out in a breathless voice, he
moves clumsily into the battle.

CONTINUED

250   CONTINUED:

The wolf-man has got hold of Harley. But now the mighty hand of the monster wheels the wolf-man around. He drops the doctor and defends himself against the monster - and a terrific battle ensues - upsetting the instruments.

Stunned, Harley and Elsa look at the fight of the Titans...

CUT TO:

251   EXT. - SLUICE-GATES - MED. CLOSE

The case of dynamite explodes - and the gate bursts, releasing the water of the dam.

252   EXT. - MOUNTAINSIDE - SLUICE-GATE - (MINIATURE)

The gate bursts - and the water rushes down the mountainside toward the ruins. The full moon shines brightly from the top of the mountains.

253   EXT. - VASARIA - STREET - WIDE

From the mountains comes the ECHO of the explosion which destroyed the gate of the dam.

People rush out of their houses - Franzec - Cuno - Rudi - Varja - the Mayor... They stare toward the mountain, shouting in despair.

254   EXT. - MOUNTAIN - LONG - (MINIATURE)

The cement pillars of the gate begin to topple, bearing along a part of the mountainside in their THUNDEROUS descent.

255   EXT. - VASARIA - STREET

The CHURCH BELLS begin to RING, to arouse the people to their impending danger, while a milling crowd looks up toward the mountains fearfully.

256   EXT. - RUINS

Maleva, about to get into her carriage, has heard
the explosion. She turns and walks back toward the
ruins - without fear.
The water can be HEARD, THUNDERING toward the ruins.

257   INT. - LABORATORY - MED. CLOSE

The wolf-man and the monster in their fight to the
death - their huge bodies on the floor - each trying
desperately to get the upper hand.

258   MED. CLOSE - HARLEY AND ELSA

Harley, thinking fast, grabs Frankenstein's diary
and pulls the petrified girl toward the exit.

From afar, mounting in roaring power, the water is
HEARD approaching.

As Harley and Elsa reach the door, the floor begins
to tremble and the walls to shake. -

259   MED. CLOSE - NEAR DOOR

Harley pulls the girl through the door.
The iron-bound book drops to the ground, unnoticed
by them.
The NOISE of rocks TUMBLING, walls TOTTERING and
CRASHING, fills the air with ever-increasing uproar.
The water bursts in and begins to mount. -

260   EXT. - RUINS - MED. FULL

As Maleva sees Harley and Elsa running toward her,
while behind them, the ruins are shaking, their
foundation washed away by the ever-increasing flood.

261   EXT. - MED. CLOSE

The carriage with Maleva's horse. The animal,
frightened but unable to get free of the carriage,
kicks its hind legs against the driver's seat, trying to tear loose.

CONTINUED

261   CONTINUED:

Harley, half-carrying Elsa, puts the girl on the
back of the wagon, then quiets the horse and takes
the reins. Helping Maleva up on the seat beside
him, he snaps the whip-lash in the air and drives
away with the women.

262   INT. - LABORATORY - MED. FULL

The wolf-man and the monster are still fighting,
as the walls topple on top of them and the water
breaks into the room in great torrents.

263   EXT. - VASARIA - STREET

The crowd looking toward the spectacle in awed
silence.

264   MOUNTAIN - (MINIATURE)

The whole mountainside seems to slide - ROARING
and THUNDERING - tons of dirt and rocks tumble down-
hill.

The ruins, half-drowned under the tremendous burst
of water from the broken dam, sinks into the ground,
swallowed up by the angry earth.

A STORM ARISES, HOWLING, WHISTLING, in fury, mingling
with the THUNDER of the crashing mountainside.

265   EXT. - STREET - VASARIA - FULL

The crowd stands and stares, as into the PICTURE
gallops the horse, as fast as his old legs can carry
him, pulling the wagon with Harley, Elsa and Maleva.

266   MED. CLOSE - STREET

The horse stops, trembling. Harley jumps from the
driver's seat and half-supporting Elsa, helps her out
of the wagon.
The STORM, created by the landslide, comes HOWLING
over the roofs of the town.

CONTINUED

266   CONTINUED:

The church bells begin to ring LOUDER, shaken by
the sudden burst of WIND. Suddenly the CHIMES
begin to play: "Ueb Immer Treu Und Redlichkeit"...

267   EXT. - MOUNTAINSIDE - (MINIATURE)

The landscape is obfuscated by a huge veil of dust,
hiding the mountains.

268   EXT. - VASARIA - STREET

The people stare into the direction of the disaster.
The men reverently take off their hats.

269   CLOSE - STREET

As Harley puts his arms around Elsa, who leans
against him for protection.

270   EXT. - VASARIA - MED. FULL

Maleva touches her horse with her whip and drives
away from the crowd, unnoticed by them as they still
silently stare toward the mountain.

The CHIMES of the church bell RISE into a CHORAL.

271   EXT. - MOUNTAINSIDE - LONG - (MINIATURE) - (MUSIC
SUSTAINED)

As the dust settles, the outline of a new hill can
be seen. Where the ruins stood, there is now a
huge tomb of earth and rocks, covering the grave of
the two phantoms.

The moon sinks behind the mountain-peak, and with
her, darkness settles on the PICTURE - and we

DISSOLVE TO:

272 CLOSE - THE SWIRLING WATERS OF THE RECEDING FLOOD

carrying along a page of Frankenstein's diary.
The CAMERA MOVES CLOSE as the page dances along
on the waves - and we read in Frankenstein's clear
scientific handwriting:

> "And when I succeed in
> creating life, I shall
> be as great as God!
>
>   Frankenstein"

The page reaches a whirlpool of black water -
swirls around - a tiny white speck - then disappears
- and as the water swallows it into the darkness of
the flood -

                                        FADE OUT

                    THE END.

*On the following pages we present the original Pressbook
which was distributed to theater owners
for publicity purposes.*

FRANKENSTEIN
meets
THE WOLF MAN
UNIVERSAL PICTURE
Copyright 1942, Universal Pictures Co., Inc.

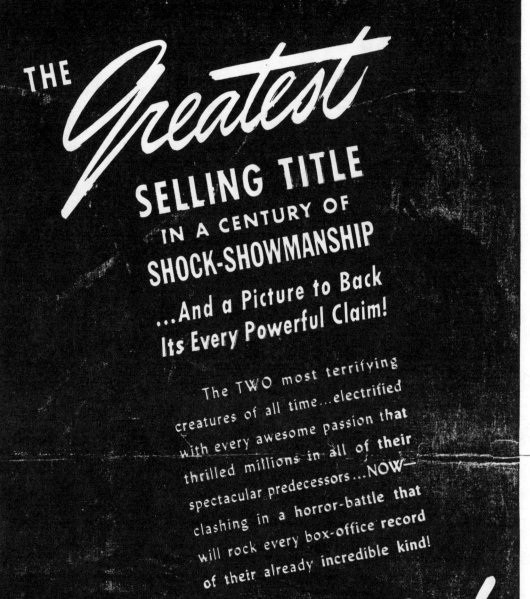

THE *Greatest* SELLING TITLE IN A CENTURY OF SHOCK-SHOWMANSHIP

...And a Picture to Back Its Every Powerful Claim!

The TWO most terrifying creatures of all time...electrified with every awesome passion that thrilled millions in all of their spectacular predecessors...NOW— clashing in a horror-battle that will rock every box-office record of their already incredible kind!

IT'S *Terror-ific!*

CASH IT IN WITH A SMASH CAMPAIGN!

CREDITS

Universal Pictures
Presents
"FRANKENSTEIN
MEETS THE WOLF MAN"
starring
ILONA MASSEY
PATRIC KNOWLES
with
Bela Lugosi, Lionel Atwill
Maria Ouspenskaya
and
LON CHANEY
in his most terrifying role
Original Screen Play.....................
...........................Curtis Siodmak
Director of Photography, George Robinson. A.S.C.: *Art Director*, John B. Goodman. *Associate*, Martin Obzina; *Director of Sound*, Bernard B. Brown. *Technician*, William Fox; *Set Decorations*, R. A. Gausman, *Associate*, E. R. Robinson; *Film Editor*, Edward Curtiss; *Gowns*, Vera West; *Musical Director*, H. J. Salter; *Assistant Director*, Melville Shyer; *Special Photographic Effects*, John P. Fulton, A.S.C.; *Make Up Artist*, Jack P. Pierce.
Directed by.....Roy William Neill
Produced by.........George Waggner

THE CAST

Baroness Elsa Frankenstein.......
..........................Ilona Massey
Dr. Mannering.......Patric Knowles
Monster ....Bela Lugosi
Mayor.........................Lionel Atwill
Maleva.............Maria Ouspenskaya
Inspector Owen..........Dennis Hoey
Franzec.......................Don Barclay
Vazec ....Rex Evans
Rudi ....Dwight Frye
Guno ....Harry Stubbs
and
LON CHANEY
as
The Wolf Man

SYNOPSIS

(Not for publication)

Larry Talbot (**Lon Chaney**), supposedly dead after being transformed into a wolf man by a gypsy curse, returns from the grave to commit a series of murders. Seeking death to end the curse, he goes to Europe to find the gypsy Maleva (**Maria Ouspenskaya**) whom he believes can help him. With Maleva, he tries to locate the Frankenstein diary which holds the key to his fate.

During the search, Larry again changes to the wolf man and in a mad attempt to escape, finds and makes friends with the Frankenstein monster. Maleva discovers them together and prevails upon Larry to return to the village. Larry wishes to buy the Frankenstein castle but Baroness Frankenstein (**Ilona Massey**) refuses to sell.

Soon after, the wolf man kills a girl. The mayor and Baroness find Larry and promise to help him die. Meanwhile, the monster becomes enraged.

Larry changes to the wolf man and grapples with the monster as a villager dynamites a dam. Quickly flood waters crash over the castle. The monster and the wolf man are caught in the swirling cataract.

2 FEROCIOUS MONSTERS TEAMED IN 'FRANKENSTEIN MEETS WOLF MAN'

Lon Chaney (Upper L.) is the Wolf Man and Bela Lugosi (Upper R.) portrays the monster in Universal's "Frankenstein Meets the Wolf Man" in which Ilona Massey and Patric Knowles are co-starred.
(Mat 11)

"Frankenstein Meets The Wolf Man," Universal's latest horror picture, has Bela Lugosi (L) in the role of the Frankenstein monster. Lon Chaney portrays the Wolf Man. Ilona Massey and Patric Knowles are co-starred in the new thrill drama.
(Mat 21)

Horror Picture Brings New Shocks Shudders

(Advance)

Two of the screen's most fearsome horror purveyors combine their wickedness to provide a double measure of chills and thrills in Universal's latest shock-film, "Frankenstein Meets the Wolf Man," coming...................to the...................Theatre. The picture, said to contain even more of the stark action drama which is credited for the success of the sensational "Frankenstein" series of films, continues the depredations of the famous monster and this time, the fiend is assisted by another frightening creation, the Wolf Man.

Spine-chilling innovations are promised in every reel of the new drama which stars Ilona Massey and Patric Knowles. Miss Massey has the role of Baroness Elsa Frankenstein, who lives under the shadow of the Frankenstein tradition. Knowles appears as Dr. Mannering, who follows the mysterious Wolf Man from one fiendish crime to another until the trail leads to the Frankenstein castle and the monster.

Bela Lugosi is seen as the monster. Others in the substantial supporting cast include Lionel Atwill and Maria Ouspenskaya. Lon Chaney portrays the Wolf Man, a role described as his most terrifying.

Monsters Revived

The story, filmed from an original screen play by Curtis Siodmak, is said to pick up the careers of the Frankenstein monster and the Wolf Man from the mysterious means by which they apparently perished in their previous movies. Their ferocity is claimed to be undiminished in the current film.

George Waggner produced "Frankenstein Meets the Wolf Man" for Universal. The picture was directed by Roy William Neill. Special photographic effects are credited to John Fulton, camera wizard, remembered for his screen achievements in the "Invisible Man" cycle of films. George Robinson is listed as Director of Photography.

Lon Chaney Terrifying In Wolf Man Disguise

(Advance)

The makeup of the Wolf Man was once considered so ultra-gruesome that for several years it lay on a shelf unused.

Jack Pierce, Universal's makeup master, disclosed this unusual fact during the filming of "Frankenstein Meets the Wolf Man" which opns...................at the...................Theatre.

Pierce was the creator of the Wolf Man makeup. It required four months of research and laboratory work, and was originally made for the "Werewolf of London," in 1934, when Henry Hull played the beast role. A less horrible makeup was used by Hull.

Used By Chaney

A number of years later the shelved Wolf Man makeup, still regarded as too gruesome, was used by Lon Chaney when he played the title role in "The Wolf Man." The public was thrilled.

Lon Chaney again dons the terrifying makeup in the present horror picture, "Frankenstein Meets the Wolf Man."

The makeup requires four hours to put on and nine hours for the transformation of a man into a wolf, which on the screen takes but a few seconds.

Noted Players Starred

Ilona Massey and Patric Knowles are co-starred in "Frankenstein Meets the Wolf Man." Bela Lugosi appears as the Monster. Lionel Atwill and Maria Ouspenskaya have important roles. The film was directed by Roy William Neill and produced by George Waggner.

SCARE PICTURE HAS MARIA OUSPENSKAYA

(Current)

Maria Ouspenskaya, who plays the role of the gypsy seer in Universal's "Frankenstein Meets the Wolf Man," was a member of the original Moscow theater in Russia, where she was born. The famous actress appears prominently in scenes with co-stars Ilona Massey and Patric Knowles in the new horror picture which is now playing at the...................Theatre. Bela Lugosi, Lionel Atwill and Lon Chaney have other leading roles.

Madame Ouspenskaya was renowned in Europe as a comedienne. She came to America in 1923 and since then has established herself as one of the screen's most capable character players.

During the filming of the horror picture she broke her leg when the horse-drawn cart in which she was riding with Chaney toppled over. Chaney also was injured.

In Hollywood, Madame Ouspenskaya operates a dramatic school.

"Frankenstein Meets the Wolf Man" was directed by Roy William Neill and produced by George Waggner.

ACTOR IN DEMAND FOR EERIE FILMS

(Current)

Film actor Dwight Frye has an unusual record. He is the only member of the "Frankenstein Meets the Wolf Man" cast to have played in all four Universal horror pictures featuring the Frankenstein monster.

In the first chiller-diller, "Frankenstein," Frye played the role of the hunchback who stole the brains which had been placed in the monster's head, and was the first man to be murdered by him.

In the current picture, now at the...................Theatre, he plays the role of Rudi, a villager.

Chills and shudders dominate the film which was made from an original screen play by Curtis Siodmak. Special photographic effects enhancing the eerie excitement of many sequences, were supplied by John P. Fulton, camera wizard.

Ilona Massey and Patric Knowles are co-starred in "Frankenstein Meets the Wolf Man." Bela Lugosi, Lionel Atwill, Maria Ouspenskaya and Lon Chaney have headline roles. The film was directed by Roy William Neill and produced by George Waggner.

◆ ◆ ◆

THRILLS PROMISED IN MOVIE SHOCKER

(Current)

Mysterious murders terrify the countryside as two of the screen's most frightening monsters go on the rampage together in Universal's latest horror picture, "Frankenstein Meets the Wolf Man," now playing at the...................Theatre.

A new array of shocks and chills serve to identify the picture as one of Hollywood's most devastating thrillers. Co-starred in leading dramatic roles are Ilona Massey and Patric Knowles. Bela Lugosi appears as the Frankenstein monster and Lon Chaney is seen as the Wolf Man. In the supporting cast are Lionel Atwill and Maria Ouspenskaya. The film was directed by Roy William Neill and produced by George Waggner.

Beautiful Ilona Massey has the leading feminine role in Universal's sensational horror-drama, "Frankenstein Meets The Wolf Man." Patric Knowles is her co-star in the shuddery picture.
(Mat 12)

PATRIC KNOWLES' CAREER STORY TOLD

(Advance)

Patric Knowles, who plays the part of Dr. Mannering in Universal's horror picture, "Frankenstein Meets the Wolf Man," got his start in theatricals at 14 when he ran away from school to join a traveling troupe. The popular young star is teamed with Ilona Massey in the new chill film which comes...................to the...................

Partic Knowles
(Mat A)

Theatre. Others in the picture are Bela Lugosi, Lionel Atwill, Maria Ouspenskaya and Lon Chaney.

Knowles was attending prep school in Oxford, England, at the time. After playing minor roles with the traveling show, he then joined the famous Abbey Players. Later he was with the Irish Repertory company, the Croydon, and the Leicester.

Motion pictures attracted him and after appearing in about 20 British films, he was signed by a Warner Bros. talent scout and brought to Hollywood.

Among the Warners pictures he played in were "The Charge of the Light Brigade," "Give Me Your Heart" and the "Adventures of Robin Hood."

Knowles is the author of a short book, "With the Wandering Players in Ireland."

His wife is the former Enid Percival, who was featured on the London stage.

Knowles' favorite sports are riding, tennis, swimming, rowing and boxing.

"Frankenstein Meets the Wolf Man" was directed by Roy William Neill and produced by George Waggner.

Bela Lugosi portrays the Frankenstein Monster in Universal's spectacular horror drama, "Frankenstein Meets The Wolf Man." Lon Chaney appears as the Wolf Man. (Mat 13)

MOST DEVASTATING HORROR PICTURE HAS ILONA MASSEY, PATRIC KNOWLES

'Frankenstein Meets The Wolf Man,' Eerie Drama

(Review)

That shuddery entertainment phenomena, the horror drama, quickens its pace and lengthens its stride in Universal's latest and most pretentious shocker, "Frankenstein Meets the Wolf Man," which enjoyed a spectacular opening yesterday at the...............Theatre. As indicated in the title, not one, but two monsters supply thrills and chills in the new picture.

In uniting the Frankenstein monster with the Wolf Man, Universal has a terrifying pair of fiends and the ingenious method by which they have been teamed by scenarist Curtis Siodmak, deserves unqualified praise. Siodmak's original screen play not only revives the Frankenstein monster and the Wolf Man from their respective tombs, but speeds them through a series of dastardly crimes which out-shock their previous cinema depredations.

Ilona Massey, co-starred with Patric Knowles, is seen as Baroness Elsa Frankenstein, current resident of the haunted Frankenstein castle where the dramatic action centers. Knowles appears as the doctor who follows the Wolf Man from one bloody tragedy to another as the killer seeks to end the gypsy curse which ultimately brings crashing destruction both to himself and his partner, the Frankenstein monster.

Lugosi In Cast

Bela Lugosi has the role of the giant monster. His difficult portrayal and fantastic makeup highlight many of the film's eerie sequences. Maria Ouspenskaya, as Maleva the gypsy, gives an ominously impressive performance and Lionel Atwill has a prominent role. Lon Chaney, known as the screen's original Wolf Man, repeats the remarkable characterization which won him distinc-

tion in the initial Wolf Man picture.

"Frankenstein Meets the Wolf Man" has been skillfully directed by Roy William Neill, while unstinted credit for its unusual fascination must be handed to Producer George Waggner. Novel and most appropriate photography was directed by cinematographer George Robinson and the special photographic effects were devised by John P. Fulton.

◆ ◆ ◆

HORROR CHAMPIONS UNITED ON SCREEN

(Advance)

Hollywood's two horror champions have been united. They are teamed in Universal's "Frankenstein Meets the Wolf Man" coming ....to the........... ....Theatre. New shocks and shudders are promised in the picture which has Ilona Massey and Patric Knowles as its co-stars.

Bela Lugosi appears as the Frankenstein monster. Lon Chaney has the Wolf Man role and others in the cast include Lionel Atwill and Maria Ouspenskaya. Roy William Neill directed "Frankenstein Meets the Wolf Man".

Glamourous and talented Ilona Massey has one of her most impressive dramatic roles in Universal's new horror picture, "Frankenstein Meets The Wolf Man." Patric Knowles is co-starred with the famous actress in the exciting chill-film. Bela Lugosi appears as the Frankenstein monster and Lon Chaney portrays the Wolf Man. Lionel Atwill and Maria Ouspenskaya have important roles in the large supporting cast. (Mat 22)

Bela Lugosi Seen As Frankenstein Monster

(Current)

The old-fashioned milkman, who got up at 3 a.m. to make deliveries, had nothing on Bela Lugosi. Recently Bela had to get up at 2:30 a.m. daily to prepare himself for his strenuous role as the monster in "Frankenstein Meets the Wolf Man," Universal's new horror picture, now at the..................Theatre.

His early morning preparations included a hot bath, then a rub-down and a half-hour rest. This was followed by massaging of cream on his face, neck, chest, hands and arms so that the ingredients used in his monster makeup would not burn or blister him.

Then came four to five hours in the hands of Jack Pierce, Universal's veteran makeup artist, to have the actor's head "built up" into the hideous features of the monster.

Next his legs were weighted heavily and geared to give that mechanical walking effect.

Seen with Lugosi in the chill drama are co-stars Ilona Massey and Patric Knowles. Others in the cast are Lionel Atwill, Maria Ouspenskaya and Lon Chaney. Roy William Neill directed.

Bela Lugosi (Mat B)

WOLF MAN PORTRAYAL SHRINKS FILM ACTOR

(Current)

Lon Chaney was six pounds lighter after nine hours in making a movie scene which shows him changing from a man to a wolf—and it all was for naught.

The young actor's weight-losing experience occurred at Universal studio in Hollywood during the production of "Frankenstein Meets the Wolf Man" now being shown at the...........................Theatre. Ilona Massey and Patric Knowles are co-starred in the new horror picture which features Bela Lugosi, Lionel Atwill and Maria Ouspenskaya. Chaney has one of the key roles.

A mechanical defect in the camera necessitated shooting the transformation over again.

In "Frankenstein Meets the Wolf Man," Chaney is required to transform at least three times into a wolf.

◆ ◆ ◆

MONSTER STRIKES BLOW AT ENEMIES

(Advance)

The enemy powers have much more to fear in the monster, played by Bela Lugosi in Universal's "Frankenstein Meets the Wolf Man," than will the moviegoers who wish to be thrilled by the gruesome scenes. The new horror picture, in which Lugosi is seen with co-stars Ilona Massey and Patric Knowles, comes.....................to the...............................Theatre.

Lugosi, while the picture was being filmed, organized the 10,000 Hungarians in the Los Angeles area into the American Hungarian Defense Federation for the battle against the so-called "new order."

The Los Angeles Hungarians donated $1600 to the Red Cross, bought $65,000 in war bonds in one day and have raised funds to buy and completely equip an ambulance for the American forces.

"Frankenstein Meets The Wolf Man," Universal's latest horror drama, has Bela Lugosi (L) in the role of the fearsome Frankenstein monster. Lon Chaney portrays the Wolf Man. (Mat 23)

MARIA OUSPENSKAYA SEEKS COMEDY ROLES

(Current)

Maria Ouspenskaya, great Russian actress, who plays the role of the gypsy seer in Universal's "Frankenstein Meets the Wolf Man," now at the....................Theatre, once gave Europe hearty laughs in comedy roles. In Russia, especially, she was renowned as a comedienne.

"Alas," says the actress, "it makes me weep at times when I realize that here in America no one will cast me in comedy. I reached the heights in comedy in Europe. Maybe some day I'll do comedy parts here."

American audiences, however, seem to prefer Maria in the type of role she has in "Frankenstein Meets the Wolf Man." In the new horror picture she is seen with co-stars Ilona Massey and Patric Knowles. Other celebrities in the film are Bela Lugosi, Lionel Atwill and Lon Chaney. The picture was directed by Roy William Neill.

BELA LUGOSI, LON CHANEY SCORE IN 'FRANKENSTEIN MEETS WOLF MAN'

Extraordinary Horror Film Has Ilona Massey

(Advance)

Ilona Massey is the coveted beauty in "Frankenstein Meets the Wolf Man," the Universal horror picture which opens ....at the........................Theatre. The tall, blonde Hungarian actress, who, before coming to Hollywood was the toast of the Viennese State Opera, is said to give one of her most impressive performances in the new chill film.

Being the mystery woman on the screen is not new to Miss Massey. Her portrayals of such characters in "Invisible Agent" and "International Spy" are well remembered.

Miss Massey came to Hollywood in 1936. Knowing no English, she was obliged to devote two long years to its study. Then, in "Rosalie," she was given a small part. In "Balalaika," she had the leading role, singing opposite Nelson Eddy. Miss Massey established herself as a star. Since then she has become one of the favorite actresses and has been given numerous dramatic roles.

Ilona Massey (Mat C)

Miss Massey is an accomplished sportswoman, being proficient in swimming, horseback riding, badminton and golf. In "Frankenstein Meets the Wolf Man," she is co-starring with Patric Knowles. Bela Lugosi, Lionel Atwill, Maria Ouspenskaya and Lon Chaney are other celebrities in the large cast. The picture was directed by Roy William Neill. George Waggner was the producer.

◆ ◆ ◆

LIONEL ATWILL HAS ROLE IN CHILL-FILM

(Advance)

Lionel Atwill, who plays the part of the mayor in Universal's horror-thriller, "Frankenstein Meets the Wolf Man," which opens ....at the........................ Theatre, for the last few years has been a top line performer in motion pictures.

Atwill, when he was a boy, yearned to be a surgeon, but he was steered into a course on architecture, and after three years of it he became more interested in theatricals.

In London he applied for a role at the Garrick Theater in "The Walls of Jericho." He got it, and from then on the theater was his choice. His debut in motion pictures was in "The White-Faced Fool."

Ilona Massey and Patric Knowles are co-starred in "Frankenstein Meets the Wolf Man." Bela Lugosi appears as the monster and Lon Chaney portrays the Wolf Man.

Bela Lugosi (L) appears as the Frankenstein monster in Universal's current horror production, "Frankenstein Meets The Wolf Man." Lon Chaney portrays the terrifying Wolf Man. (Mat 24)

Premature Burial Basis Of Shuddery Movie Plot

(Advance)

That the dead may come back to life, as depicted in horror motion pictures, is a possibility and not so fantastic as many believe, research records disclosed during the production of "Frankenstein Meets the Wolf Man" at Universal studio in Hollywood. The new shudder drama co-starring Ilona Massey and Patric Knowles comes........................to the........................ Theatre. Bela Lugosi, Lionel Atwill, Maria Ouspenskaya and Lon Chaney have key dramatic roles.

Human bodies, it was revealed, can be put in storage, frozen for long periods, and be brought back to life.

Medical books cite numerous cases where people have relapsed into hibernation, and their bodies have shown no signs of life.

Authorities have contended that this is possible, for prehistoric man, like the beast, was supposedly gifted with the mental facilities to hibernate through the long, bitterly cold winter months.

In December, 1935, Dr. Alexis Carrel, Nobel prize winner and a member of the Rockefeller Institute, asserted in a lecture on "Mystery of Death," that "although remote, some individuals could be put in storage for long periods of time, brought back to normal existence for other periods, and permitted in this manner to live for centuries."

Dr. Edward P. Vollum, a surgeon in the U. S. Army, reported in a research paper that there are forms of suspension of life which could defy the highest medical skill and he listed trance, autohypnotism, somnambulism and hibernation among them.

Monster Frozen

In "Frankenstein Meets the Wolf Man," Bela Lugosi, in the role of the monster, is frozen in ice, chopped out and revived; Lon Chaney, in the role of the Wolf Man, is supposedly dead for some time and entombed, but when two grave robbers pry open the stone coffin, they find him alive.

In 1919 the German medical profession investigated an extraordinary case, which, after careful examination, was listed as hibernation for "some months."

Lon Chaney who portrays the Wolf Man in Universal's "Frankenstein Meets The Wolf Man," is pictured here with his famous police dog, "Moose." (Mat 15)

HISTORY OF MOVIE MONSTER REVEALED

(Current)

Conceiving and creating the monster in "Frankenstein Meets the Wolf Man," the Universal horror picture now at the........................ Theatre, required a half-year of tedious research and laboratory work.

Jack Pierce, Universal's makeup exponent, was the originator. For two months he studied the possibility of such a man-made monstrosity, then he did research work, consulting scientists, and surgeons.

Pierce explains that his research carried him to libraries having ancient Egyptian scrolls and volumes dealing with people who were buried alive.

Pierce created the monster in 1932 for the Universal horror picture, "Frankenstein."

Former Hits Recalled

Boris Karloff had the role, and again in "The Bride of Frankenstein," made in 1935, and in "The Son of Frankenstein" in 1939.

Lon Chaney was the monster in "The Return of Frankenstein" in 1941.

Bela Lugosi plays it in this latest horror picture, "Frankenstein Meets the Wolf Man." The makeup requires four hours' time to apply.

Ilona Massey and Patric Knowles are co-starred in "Frankenstein Meets the Wolf Man."

Other notables in the large cast are Lionel Atwill and Maria Ouspenskaya. Lon Chaney appears as the "Wolf Man."

Curtis Siodmak authored the original screen play which is said to contain even more shuddery sequences than the previous "Frankenstein" horror movies. Photography was directed by George Robinson with special effects contributed by John P. Fulton, famous for the remarkable "Invisible Man" screen illusions.

Roy William Neill directed and George Waggner produced the new chill and shock movie.

Ilona Massey and Patric Knowles are co-starred in Universal's most pretentious horror film, "Frankenstein Meets The Wolf Man." (Mat 14)

HORROR, HARD WORK CLAIMS LON CHANEY

(Current)

The grass on the other side of the fence looks greener—even to the stars of the movie world out in Hollywood!

Lon Chaney (Mat D)

Take Lon Chaney for instance. He groans when he has to don hideous picture makeup. Chaney yearns for the Charles Boyer type of roles. And you can't blame Chaney much, for the horror adornments are tedious and painful.

In Universal's latest chiller-diller, "Frankenstein Meets the Wolf Man," now at the........................ Theatre, Chaney had to spend four hours putting on the Wolf Man makeup early in the morning. The transformation of the actor into the beast, which requires only five seconds on the screen, consumed nine hours of hard work before the camera.

"When I got my break in pictures, in 'Of Mice and Men,' I was Lennie, the imbecile," Chaney moaned, "Now, I'm typed as an ideal horror-man. I scare women and children and give the men shudders."

Ilona Massey and Patric Knowles are co-starred in "Frankenstein Meets the Wolf Man." Other favorites in the cast are Bela Lugosi, Lionel Atwill and Maria Ouspenskaya. The new chill drama was directed by Roy William Neill.

Home-towns, Birthdays of Players

Ilona Massey	Budapest, Hungary	July 16
Patric Knowles	Yorkshire, England	Nov. 11
Bela Lugosi	Lugos, Hungary	Oct. 20
Lionel Atwill	Croyden, England	March 1
Maria Ouspenskaya	Tula, Russia	Dec. 28
Lon Chaney	Oklahoma City, Okla.	Feb. 10

Showmanship!

DISPLAY LINES

The screen rocks to the shock of its greatest sensation—TWIN MONSTER HORROR SHOW!

The shock-battle of the century — fiend of fury battling a night-born killer. ALL NEW THRILLS!

A hundred times more terrifying, as these TITANS OF TERROR clash in mortal combat.

MONSTERS AMUCK! Inhuman beasts raging with fury! The greatest DOUBLE HORROR SHOW of them all . . . FRANKENSTEIN AND THE WOLF MAN . . . BOTH IN ONE PICTURE!

★ ★ ★

SCRIM SHADOWBOX

With the aid of a scrim, and light bulbs, lobby display presents first the figure of "Frankenstein", then "Wolf Man". Lighting arrangement of both figures and copy emphasizes your big selling point of a *double-monster picture.*

With art work, or photographic blowups, mount two upright figures of Frankenstein and Wolf Man facing each other in a shadowbox. Run a strip of compo down the middle, separating them. Add masked lights along top and sides.

Or, in place of opaque blowups or paintings with lights in front of them, have sign shop make transparencies that are lit up from behind.

Letter the name "FRANKENSTEIN" over that figure. Letter the name "WOLF MAN" over the second figure. Cover front of box with a piece of scrim. Letter the word "MEETS" on separate card and place this in the center and over scrim. Arrange your lights so that when the "Frankenstein" panel is lighted, the "Wolf Man" panel is not, and vice versa. So far as your copy is concerned, the only word that is permanently in view is the word "MEETS".

Page Six

EFFECTIVE POSTER CUTOUTS

The huge fighting figures of Frankenstein and The Wolf Man reproduced on the 24-sheet make fine cut-out material for top of your marquee. Sign shop can easily paint over the small portion of the title which covers a part of Frankenstein. Use an opaque paint of matching color and the spotting will never be noticed. Cut out the letters in the title and mount in a shadowbox, each letter covered in light green cellophane, with flasher lights behind. Flasher circuit should first light up the word "Frankenstein," then "Meets," then "The Wolf Man," hold all for a few seconds, then go blank and repeat the "travel." Light the fighting figures in green also, but use a bright white spot-light on the girl. Cut the contrasting lights as sharply as possible, by taping across the upper half of the spot used on the girl. The effect should make the fighting figures more eerie than solid lighting would produce.

Make two cutouts from the six-sheet, one of Ilona Massey, and one of the fighting figures and title. Place in your foyer for an advance, in such a way that patrons see the girl first; her pose will cause them to look up in the direction she is looking. Some place along this line of vision place the cutout fighting figures. The ideal place is along a stairway to the mez, if your house has one.

★ ★ ★

"FUR" and "METAL" BANNER

Play up the "mechanical man" and "animal" angle by reproducing the title in "metal" and "animal fur", across an advance banner. Sign shop builds the word "Frankenstein" out of wood or compo block letters and paints it silver to suggest metal. Add large headed nails to look like rivets. General appearance is similar to sketch herewith.

For the word "Wolf Man", use cut-out compo as a base for your letters. Get scraps of cheap fur from a local furrier (they usually have bits that are too small for any practical use). If you can't get real fur, sign shop can imitate it with finely frayed rope ends or with cotton batting that is combed out and sprayed brown.

TEASING THE WORD "LYCANTHROPE"

LYCANTHROPE. 1. Folklore. A werwolf. 2. One afflicted with lycanthrophy . . . LYCANTHROPHY. 1. The fabulous powers of transformation of a human being into a wolf. Belief in werwolves . . . A mania in which the patient imagines himself to be a wolf . . . FUNK & WAGNALLS DICTIONARY.

You can use this word to good advantage for a series of "word" teasers in newspaper or in your lobby or in showcards placed in windows around town. Below are suggested teaser lines:

LYCANTHROPY

A Word To Shudder Over!

when "Frankenstein Meets The Wolf Man" on (date)

LYCANTHROPHY

The Old Legend Says It Is Dangerous, to Pronounce These Letters Too Much!

You'll know why when "Frankenstein Meets The Wolf Man" (date)

I AM A "LYCANTROPE"

Repeat it thus, under the Full Moon Yet take care, there is Wolfbane in Thy Hand!

(And see "Frankenstein Meets The Wolf Man" (date)

LYCANTHROPHY

Like an Evil Dream Come True!

("Frankenstein Meets The Wolf Man" (date)

LYCANTHROPE

It's foul meaning is shrouded in shuddering shadows under a monsterous moon!

when "Frankenstein Meets The Wolf Man" (date)

LYCANTHROPHY

It will be thy good fortune Never, never, to know It's Meaning!

until "Frankenstein Meets The Wolf Man" (date)

LYCANTHROPE

Horrible harpy of the Imagination Or Scientific Truth?

You'll know, when "Frankenstein Meets The Wolf Man" (date)

LYCANTHROPHY

Some say it's so Others, say no!

It's the weirdest word ever spoken when "Frankenstein Meets The Wolf Man" (date)

★ ★ ★

LIVE SHOCK AD

Place a large glass display case on a hospital table. Station a girl in nurse's white uniform beside it. In the case put small bottles of smelling salts and offer them for sale at regular retail prices. You can secure these on consignment from your druggist. Add signs reading:

BE PREPARED FOR THE SHOCK OF YOUR LIFE!
SMELLING SALTS, 25c
GOOD FOR WHAT SCARES YOU!

TITLE-TEASERS

For use in newspapers. Another good use for teaser copy is to have sign shop letter it on a number of cards for spotting in windows around town and for sniping wherever the cards can be tacked up. Following are suggested lines:

MOST MONSTEROUS MEETING IN MOTION PICTURES!

At last . . . "F" MEETS "W" (date)

IMMOVABLE OBJECT MEETS IRRESISTIBLE FORCE!

(date) WHEN "F" MEETS "W"

WEIRDEST MEETING IN HISTORY!

"F" MEETS "W" on (date)

THEY'RE COMING TOGETHER (date)!

"F" MEETS "W"

THE COLLISION OF THE CENTURY!

"F" MEETS "W" on (date)

TWO MONSTERS MEET IN DOUBLE-HORROR "FRANKENSTEIN MEETS THE WOLF MAN" (date)

At the Blank Theatre

Silk Screen Accessories

Smashing . . . Eye Catching . . . Attractive! 40x60, 30x40, 24x60 and other types of Specialty Accessories available and on display for Universal Pictures. at your local NATIONAL SCREEN EXCHANGE.

MAX FACTOR CAMPAIGN

Max Factor releases an Ilona Massey ad. for FEBRUARY in American magazines. This particular ad. gives a tremendous break clear across the top of the ad. (see illustration) to "Frankenstein Meets The Wolf Man".

Clip copies of this ad. from February magazines and mount as the center piece of special Max Factor tie-up windows in drug and department stores. In instances of high class windows, blow up the ad. into a sepia enlargement. As an exchange courtesy promote yourself a real window by offering to exhibit a blowup of the ad. on a small table in your lobby flanked by an exhibit of Max Factor products.

Add to your tie-up displays stills from your Exchange Set featuring Ilona Massey.

★　★　★

Sell the 2 IN 1 Angle

In having Frankenstein and The Wolf Man in one picture you have the biggest thing in horror shows yet conceived. It's a TWO IN ONE horror show. Play it up with teasers and snipes long before you begin your regular campaign. Reproduce the two figures, and use ad-lines capitalizing on this double monster attraction:

TWO HORROR SHOWS IN ONE

TWICE THE THRILLS WITH TWICE AS MANY MONSTERS

BEWARE OF THE DAY "FRANKENSTEIN MEETS THE WOLF MAN"

CAN YOU STAND A *DOUBLE* SHOCK?

SILK BANNER

Monsters' Hide-Out Contest

A contest along the line, "Where would Frankenstein and the Wolf Man hide in your town" has good possibilities. Every town seems to have its haunted house or eerie corner. Contest can either call for photos or letters describing the spot. The thought of monsters roaming home town streets will bring the picture "home" to local news readers, and start imaginations working—all of which builds an interest that can be satisfied only by seeing the picture. You'll likely get several gag answers, like: "They'd hide in Greasy Joe's Restaurant," and if you want you can play this angle by photographing a few gag spots and displaying them along with the other photos and letters you receive. Offer free admission for each "hide-out" displayed in your lobby, with possibly a cash prize for the top entries.

★　★　★

ACCESSORY ORDER

"Frankenstein Meets The Wolf Man"

ITEMS	Unit Price	Quantity	Amount
One Sheet	.15 ea.		
Three Sheet	.45 ea.		
Six Sheet	.90 ea.		
24 Sheet	2.40 ea.		
22x28	.40 ea.		
Eight 11x14's	.75 set		
14x36 Insert	.25 ea.		
Midget Window Card	.03½ ea.		
Regular Window Card	.07 ea.		
40x60 Gelatin	1.00 ea.		
6x9 One-Color Herald	2.25 M.		
Silk Banner	1.75 ea.		
Regular 8x10 Stills	.10 ea.		
		TOTAL	

Manager....................

Theatre....................

Address....................

6x9 HERALD ONE COLOR $2.25 PER M.

TITANS OF TERROR! *Clashing in Mortal Combat!*

Twice as grim! A hundred times more terrifying! ALL NEW THRILLS...as the screen rocks to the shock of its greatest sensation!

FRANKENSTEIN *meets* **THE WOLF MAN**

Ilona MASSEY　Patric KNOWLES

with Bela LUGOSI　Lionel ATWILL　Maria OUSPENSKAYA

and LON CHANEY IN HIS MOST TERRIFYING ROLE

Original Screen Play, Curtis Siodmak　Directed by ROY WILLIAM NEILL　Produced by GEORGE WAGGNER　A UNIVERSAL PICTURE

POSTERS ✶ ✶ ✶ ✶

TWENTY-FOUR

THREE

EIGHT 11 x 14's

ONE 22 x 28

SIX

ONE

40 x 60

14 x 36

IMPRINT SPACE

ADDED ATTRACTIONS

REGULAR WINDOW CARD

MIDGET WINDOW CARD

IMPRINT SPACE

A UNIVERSAL PICTURE 1B
Ad No. 1B—1 Col.—Mat 15c

Original Screen Play, Curtis Siodmak
Directed by ROY WILLIAM NEILL
Produced by GEORGE WAGGNER
A UNIVERSAL PICTURE 1G
Ad No. 1G—1 Col.—Mat 15c

Ad No. 1F—1 Col.—Mat 15c

A UNIVERSAL PICTURE 2C
Ad No. 2C—2 Col.—Mat 30c

Ad No. 1D—1 Col.—Mat 15c

Ad No. 2A—2 Col.—Mat 30c

Ad No. 1C—1 Col.—Mat 15c

Ad No. 1E—1 Col.—Mat 15c

FIEND OF FURY
vs. NIGHT-BORN KILLER!
ALL NEW THRILLS!

The Titans of Terror
unleashed...in the shock-
battle of the century!

FRANKENSTEIN
meets
THE WOLF MAN

starring
ILONA MASSEY   **PATRIC KNOWLES**

with
BELA LUGOSI   **LIONEL ATWILL**
MARIA OUSPENSKAYA

and
LON CHANEY
in his most terrifying role!

UNIVERSAL

Directed by ROY WILLIAM NEILL   **A UNIVERSAL PICTURE**   Produced by GEORGE WAGGNER
Original Screen Play, Curtis Siodmak

3A

The studio cutting continuity for the preview trailer* of *Frankenstein Meets the Wolf Man*

(A cutting continuity is provided by the editors of a film, usually under the supervision of the director. Its purpose is to show the actual film-on-paper, providing the scene, action and how many feet of film comprise each scene. With the Universal horror films experiencing a world-wide revival due to MCA/UNIVERSAL HOME VIDEO, these continuities are the most important documents for film labs, as they are the only record in existence of how the films appeared when they were originally released.)

DIALOGUE CONTINUITY

T R A I L E R

"FRANKENSTEIN MEETS THE WOLF MAN"

Starring

ILONA MASSEY
PATRIC KNOWLES

With

LIONEL ATWILL
BELA LUGOSI
MARIA OUSPENSKYA
DENNIS HOEY

And
LON CHANEY
as the Wolf Man

FEBRUARY 4, 1943

PICTURE NO. 1279
DIRECTOR NEILL

*A Preview Trailer is another word for "Coming Attractions" shorts, shown before the main feature at the time.

PICTURE NO. 1279
DIRECTOR NEILL
PAGE ONE

DIALOGUE & CONTINUITY

TRAILER

ON

"FRANKENSTEIN MEETS THE WOLF MAN"

1. VIEW IN GRAVEYARD
   Camera cranes back - three
   men crossing graveyard -   MUSIC THROUGHOUT REEL
   Words come on -

   PREPARE FOR THE SHOCK OF YOUR LIFE!

   Words exit -

   ......JAGGED OPENING WIPE TO

   LARGE CLOSE UP MONSTERS FACE
   Word comes on -

          FRANKENSTEIN

   Word exits -

   .....OPENING JAGGED WIPE TO

   LARGE CLOSE UP THE WOLF MAN
   Word comes on -

          MEETS

   Word exits - others come in -

          THE WOLF MAN

   Words exit -

   ...JAGGED WIPE TO

   VIEW ON VILLAGE STREET
   Crowd of towns fold carrying
   lamps and guns marching across
   street -
   Words come on -

   --to overwhelm you with HORROR...
          twice as grim

   Words exit -

PAGE TWO

2. CLOSE SHOT ON STREET
   Monster approaching camera -
   Words come on -

   a hundred times more terryifying!

   Words exit -

3. MED. CLOSE SHOT ON STREET
   Monster crossing from b.g. -
   arms outstretched -group of   SCREAMS
   girls come running around
   horses - girls terrified -

4. CLOSE SHOT GROUP OF TOWNSFOLD
   Moving across - terrified -

5. CLOSE SHOT STREET
   Townsfold running on past
   Larry near arbor and exit -
   Larry runs onto street -
   camera moves - he grabs the
   Monster - shakes his arm -

   ...OPENING JAGGED WIPE TO

   CLOSE VIEW INT. HOSPITAL ROOM
   Larry in bed - leaning on his
   elbows - talking to Doctor and
   Inspector standing at foot of
   bed - camera moves up close -

          LARRY - But he doesn't understand
          There's a curse upon me. I
          change into a wolf.

7. VIEW OF LAB IN RUINS
   Doctor at work on machinery -
   Elsa stands center f.g.   NOISE OF MACHINERY
   watching sparks from machinery -

8. CLOSE UP ELSA
   Looking off terrified -

          ELSA YELLS - Frank? Frank!'

PAGE THREE

9. VIEW IN LAB
   Doctor and Elsa as before -
   machinery giving off sparks -   SOUND OF MACHINERY
   Doctor -

10. CLOSE UP IN LAB
    Elsa approaches Doctor -
    holds his arm - looks into
    his face - talks- gravely -

          ELSA - Listen to me - I saw my
          father become obsessed by his
          power. He died a horrible
          death.

   ...JAGGED LOWER WIPE TO

   CLOSE SHOT OF GROUP OF TOWNSMEN

   Mayor and others close in
   around Vasec - Mayor speaks to
   Vasec -   CROWD YELLS

          MAYOR - There's no need for us all
          to storm after her. She'll
          come in if I ask.

          VASEC - Why should we treat her
          so fancy? She's a Frankenstein.

11. CLOSE UP LAB
    Monster picks Elsa up -
    starts walking with her -

12. CLOSE ON WOLF MAN
    Scowling - breaks loose his
    bonds -

13. VIEW IN RUINED LAB
    Monster carrying Elsa - mount-
    ing steps in far b.g. - Wolf
    Man rushes across after him.

14. CLOSE RUINED LAB
    Monster carrying Elsa to f.g. -
    Wolf Man attacks him from the
    rear - Monster drops Elsa -

15. LONG SHOT TO CASTLE AND DAM
    Explosion occurs - dam breaks -
    debris flies -

PAGE FOUR

16. CLOSE UP IN LAB
    Monster and Wolf Man fighting
    Words come on -

    Mighty monsters locked in
    mortal combat...

    Words exit -

17. MED FULL SHOT IN RUINS
    Avalanche of water bursts on -
    Words come on -
    Starring Bela Lugosi as
          The Monster

          Lon Chaney as
          The Wolf Man

    Words exit

    ...JAGGED OPENING WIPE TO

    CLOSE UP ELSA AND THE DOCTOR
    Both look off - horrified -
    Names come on -

          and Ilona Massey
          Patric Knowles

    Words continue -

18. CLOSE UP IN WOODS
    Man searching -
    Words come on -

          with
          Lionel Atwill
          Maria Ouspenskaya
          Dennis Hoey

    Words exit -

19. CLOSE SHOT CAVE
    Larry f.g. facing Monster -
    Title comes on -

    FRANKENSTEIN MEETS THE WOLF MAN

          A UNIVERSAL HORROR HIT

DS:JF

Appendix

A few years after completing *Frankenstein Meets the Wolf Man*, Bela Lugosi filled out the following questionnaire. We find it important to the fans of Mr. Lugosi to include it in this volume because of the valuable information about his life. The following pages are in Mr. Lugosi's own hand. (Courtesy Samuel S. Sherman)

CAMEO PICTURES CORPORATION
BIOGRAPHICAL INFORMATION

PART OF:
IN:

This is to insure accuracy in our publicity, and to provide complete and accurate material necessary for newspaper and magazine stories.

1. Screen name _Bela Lugosi_ Real name in full _WAS Bela BlAsko -legally changed-to- Bela Lugosi_

2. Height _6' 1"_ Nickname _NoNe_

3. Nationality _HuNgARiaN_ Color of hair _BROWN_

   Weight _170 lbs._ Color of eyes _Blue_

4. Birthplace _Lugos, Hungary_ Date _October 20, 1888_

5. Education _____ Highschool _____ College _✓_

6. Parents names _Stephen BlAsko - (FAther) TAylA (Mother)_ Both living? _no_

   Where _BuRRied at Lugos, HuNgARy VoN VojNics_ Father's business _WAS - BANK PresideNt_

   Famous ancestors or relatives _NoNe_

   Brothers or sisters names _VilmA - HAjos - LAszlo_

   Earliest childhood ambition _HighwAy BANdit_

7. Present ambition _Dude RANch_

8. First occupation _ActoR._ Where? _TRAvelling RepeRtoiRe_

   Past and present business interests apart from the screen _NoNe_

9. How did your career begin? (Amateur shows, college dramatics, beauty contests, started by famous actor or director, for a lark)

   College DRAmAtics

10. Stage debut in _Romeo_ Year _1906_ Place _Lugosi- HuNgARy_

    Broadway debut _Red Poppy_ Year _1923_ Starred with Estelle _co_

    Last play _MuRdeR-in-the- UANities_ Year _1933_ Place _New YoRk City- WyNN Wood_

    Other important plays _In AmeRicA - "DRAculA"_

    IN HuNgARy - All- the gReAt pARts iN liteRAtuRe

    Stock in what cities _NoNe_

11. Film debut in _"The SileNt CommANd"_ Year _1923_ Star _HeAvy - with AN All stAR cAst_

    First large part in _SAme_ Year _-_ Star _-_

    First talkie _"PRisoNeRs"_ Year _1929_ Star _CoRiNNe GRiffith_

    Last picture _MARk of the VampiRes_ Year _1935_ Star _All STAR At - M.G.M._

    Other pictures (Next to last, etc.) _"MysteRious MR. WoNg"_

    "RetuRN of ChANdu" - "BlAck CAt" -

12. Favorite Screen role __"Count Dracula"__ in "__Dracula__"

13. Favorite Stage role __Cyrano de Bergerac__ in __Cyrano de Bergerac__

14. Prefer screen to stage? __yes__   Why __Variety__

15. What type of role have you played most? __great characters__

16. What type do you prefer __Human interest__

17. Favorite stage players __None__

18. Favorite screen players __None Mickey Mouse__

19. Favorite playrights __—__

20. Favorite books __Social Science and Economy__

21. Favorite authors __none -__

22. Favorite sports to watch __Soccer__

23. Favorite sports to play __Golf__

24. HIGHSPOTS of your life (in chronological order)

        1 to 10 years __) it is__

        10 to 20 years __{ No ones business__

        20 to 30 years __)__

        Ad infinitum

25. CLOTHES prefer conservative or modish
              ready made or tailored __conservative tailored__

    Favor sports or formal wear? __Sports__

    Favorite colors __bright__

    Favorite materials __flannels__

26. Have you any beauty secrets such as methods of make-up, care of
    hair, eyes, hands, skin, facials, massages, oils, creams?

    __None__

27. How do you keep in condition? (Health institute, daily or weekly
    massages, sun-baths, setting-up exercises, sports?) __e.it.__

28. FOOD favorite dish __Stuffed Cabbage__ Like to cook? __—__

    Between meal snacks __no__   Bedtime snack? __no__

    Favorite recipe: Dish:

29. Married? *Yes* ___ Or want to be? _____ To whom? _____

   Date *Jan. 31- 1933* _____ Children? _____

   Favorite type of man or woman *Reserved and Honest* _____

30. What do you do for diversion and recreation aside from sports?
   (Dance, sing, write, paint, compose music, sclup, read, games)

   _____

31. Where do you prefer to live permanently?
   (Seashore, mountains, city, abroad) _____

32. Where do you live now? (Apartment, House, seashore, city,

   mountains?) _____

33. Where have you traveled? *All over the world*

34. Who are your closest friends? *Stage Hands*

35. What makes you angry? *Talk*

36. What pets have you? *3 Dogs*

37. What do you do on the set? *Smoke*

38. Where do you go week-ends? *Outing*

39. Do you own any cars, airplanes, yachts, horses? *Car*

40. Interested in politics? *Yes*

41. Pet peeves *Aggravation* ___ Live with parents? *No*

42. Pet economy *Matches + Corks* ___ Pet extravagance *Old Wines and Good Cigars*

43. Favorite dress ___ Favorite perfume *Eau de Cologne*

44. DO YOU SMOKE? *Yes* ___ Speak any foreign language? *Hungarian and others*

45. Your greatest thrill *When I got aboard ship to come to America*

46. DO YOU LIKE

   Autographs? *No* ___ Rain? *No* To write letters? *No*

   Night clubs? *No* ___ Animals *Yes* To pose for stills *No*

   Street cars? *No* ___ Children *Yes* ___ To carry umbrellas *No*

   Prohibition? *No* ___ Sun baths? *Yes* Showers or bathtubs *both*

   To entertain *Yes* Fan mail *Yes* ___ Modern architecture *Yes*

   To sleep late? *Yes* ___ Holidays *?* ___ Personal appearances *No*

   Silk underwear *No* Premiers *No* To drive your own car *No*

   Radio programs *No* ___ To dine at home *Yes* Open cars *No*

   To go shopping? *Yes* Airplanes *No* To read before sleeping *Yes*

   Ice cream cones *No* Bathsalts *No* ___ Letters of introduction?

   No To travel alone? *Yes* Hollywood *Yes* Bright ~~or subdued~~ colors

The editor gratefully acknowledges the assistance and contributions provided by the following individuals in the preparation of this series over the past 20 years:

Bud Abbott (Late)
Patty Andrews
Lew Ayres
William Bakewell
Ralph Bellamy
Stanley Bergerman
Robert Bloch
Richard Bojarski
Lincoln Bond
Ronald Borst
David Bradley
Kevin Brownlow
Ivan Butler
James Cagney (Late)
John Carradine (Late)
Ben & Anne Carre
Jeffrey Carrier
Ronald Chaney
Lon Chaney Jr. (Late)
Carlos Clarens (Late)
Mae Clarke
Franklin Coen
Ned Comstock
Mary Corliss
James Curtis
Nancy Cushing-Jones
Robert Cushman
Walter Daugherty
Gary Dorst
Todd Feiertag
Bramwell Fletcher (Late)
Robert Florey (Late)
A. Arnold Gillespie (Late)
Curtis Harrington
Patricia Hitchcock
Valerie Hobson
Bob Hope
David S. Horsley (Late)
Henry Hull (Late)
Paul Ivano (Late)
Steven Jochsberger (Late)
Zita Johann
Raymond F. Jones
Boris Karloff (Late)
John Kobal
Carl Laemmle Jr.
Carla Laemmle
Elsa Lanchester (Late)
John Landis
Janet Leigh
Celia Lovsky
Arthur Lubin
Rouben Mamoulian (Late)
Paul Mandell

Howard Mandlebaum
Gregory Mank
David Manners
Lester Matthews
John McLaughlin
Scott McQueen
Patsy Ruth Miller
Jeff Morrow
Gary Pasternak
Jim Pepper
Anthony Perkins
Mary Philbin
Armando Ponce
Vincent Price
Dr. Donald Reed
William Rosar
Margaret Ross
Hans J. Salter
Anne Schlosser
Martin Scorsese
Sherry Seeling
Wes Shank
Curt Siodmak
Robert Skotak
Joseph Stephano
James Stewart
Glenn Strange (Late)
Kenneth Strickfaden (Late)
George Turner
Edward Van Sloan (Late)
Elena Verdugo
Marc Wanamaker
Dan Woodruff
Wallace Worsley Jr.
and
FORREST J ACKERMAN, Founder of the Ackerman Archives. During the early 30s, FJA had exchanged 62 letters with Carl Laemmle Sr. As a result, Mr. Laemmle on his President's stationery, wrote a note to whom it may concern saying, in effect, "Give this young man anything he wants." As a consequence, the young Forry Ackerman acquired stills, posters, pressbooks, and the sound discs from FRANKENSTEIN, THE MUMMY, THE OLD DARK HOUSE and MURDERS IN THE RUE MORGUE. Since that date, the collection has grown to hundreds of thousands of items dealing with the classic Universal films, and items from the Science Fiction and Fantasy genre. We are indeed fortunate to have this wonderland of memorabilia as our foundation. Nearly 60 years later, almost to the word, Universal Studios has granted Philip J. Riley, one of Ackerman's former assistants, and MagicImage Filmbooks the same gift in recognition of their concern and realization of Universal's great heritage in the art of Motion Picture Production. Combined with the talents and contributions of those named above, we pledge to produce the highest quality historic works, so that future generations may benefit from firsthand knowledge of the magical city of Hollywood which created a new art form - and unknowingly protected the greatest gift of our childhood - the imagination.